MW00637888

The Great Chefs of BALTIMORE

Barbara Tasch Ezratty, editor

www.omnititles.com

The Great Chefs of Baltimore
ISBN: 0942929-23-3

Send all inquiries to:
Omni Arts Publishing Inc.
133 West Read Street
Baltimore, MD 21201

Toll-free (888) 964-BOOK
http://www.omnititles.com

Book layout and design: Rich Gottesman
Omni Arts Photographer: Annie Reid-Stone
Cover art: Kevin Sherry
Drum scanning and color correction: Tse Worldwide Press
Cover design: Sutileza Graphics

Printed by Tse Worldwide Press
Los Angeles, China

The Great Chefs of BALTIMORE

Assad Akbari
Marc Attman
Antonio Baines
Nick Bates
Mike Broglio
John "Tip" Carter IV
Robert Cernak
Richard Cook
John Creger
Mimmo Cricchio
Donna Crivello
Christina D'Angelo
Christian deLutis
Luis Diaz
Rashed Edwards
Rey Eugenio
Nate Finney
Steve Francis
Russel Frew
Nino Germano
Brian Greene
Brian Hart
Edwin "Zeus" Herman
Eric Huckleberry
Troy Jones
Christopher Lewis
Dennis Marcoux

Brian Martin
Kevin Miller
Tim Mullen
Ravi Narayanan
Felix Nuñez
Paul Oliver
Chris Patternote
Renato Rotondo, Sr.
Barry Rumsey
Staci Rush
Michael Russell Jr.
Emilio Sanz
Tom Schwarzweller
John Shields
Jeffrey Smith
Ted Stelzenmuller
Bryan Sullivan
Sonny Sweetman
Franklin Thomas
Frances Thompson
Graham Weber
William Wesner
Bob Whitehead
Denise Whiting
Cindy Wolf
Eric Yeager
Joshua Young

Recipes from your favorite Maryland Chefs

Great Chefs of BALTIMORE

Photo: Annie Reid-Stone

Great Chefs of **BALTIMORE**

From the Editor

After 12 years as a restaurant reviewer and cookbook publisher in another city, I came back to Baltimore to fall in love again - with its new and old, local and ethnic, traditional and cutting-edge restaurants.

When I was growing up in Baltimore, dining out meant spaghetti and meatballs in Little Italy, hot dogs with hot bologna wrapped around them on Corned Beef Row, Chicken Chow Mein at downtown's White Rice Inn, or steamed crabs, anyplace!

And you can still get all that in Baltimore (although the White Rice Inn has long since departed). But today's restaurants offer even more than these traditional comfort foods. Our chefs – those specializing in local Chesapeake and other American cuisines, and others trained in the cuisines of Asian, European, the Caribbean, and South American countries – are also attracting and satisfying sophisticated-palate clientele, with appetites and tastes honed from coastal to coastal as well as international cuisines. And old city neighborhoods continue to attract new residents who want more varied restaurants. These new restaurants attract even more residents. It's a marvelous circle that's helping Baltimore grow.

In addition to being a vibrant dining destination, Baltimore's attractions - the Inner Harbor with its National Aquarium and the Science Center; its fascinating museums within walking distance (American Visionary Art Museum, the Museum of Industry, the Reginald Lewis African American Museum, the Jewish Museum of Maryland, the Walters Art Museum, and Oriole Park at Camden Yards with its Babe Ruth/Maryland Sports Museum, to name just a few); Convention Center, restaurants and shops is a magnet for millions of conventioneers, sport fans, and vacationing families annually. (I've heard 10 million visitors a year: could that be?! Are you one of them?) Plus, residents of Baltimore are – in keeping with national trends – eating out more frequently than ever.

The Great Chefs of Baltimore create their masterpieces in restaurants as varied as the available cuisines. Some are fine-dining restaurants where elegant surroundings and succulent foods combine to make a memorable dining experience. Others are casual restaurants where a comfortable ambiance and comfort foods let you leave feeling happily satisfied.

To entice you to visit their restaurants, the Great Chefs of Baltimore present here some of their popular recipes for you to try at home. Once you sample their cuisines, you'll want to taste more of their menus. The address of each restaurant is within these pages.

This, then, is a cookbook designed to tempt you. And if you've already visited the restaurants and are going to use this book to remember your experience, Enjoy! May you be tempted to come back to Baltimore.

Acknowledgements

This is to express my admiration to all the great chefs of Baltimore. If ever a city has experienced a Renaissance with a capital R, it is this one, and the city's chefs are in the vanguard.

In the last decade, Baltimore has seen changes for the better in its landscape, its job market, its housing options and certainly in its restaurants. As the city's population continues to increase in record numbers, and tourism continues to grow, the restaurant scene becomes more and more vibrant.

I salute all of the Great Chefs of Baltimore, who are pleasing the city's residents and visitors on a daily basis. Your expertise has made this book possible.

I thank Rich Gottesman of Sutileza Graphics, whose genius at graphic design makes our books look so good; Annie Reid-Stone for her fabulous photos; Kevin Sherry for the tempting artwork on the cover; and Lars Rusin of the "Baltimore Foodies," for his insightful introduction.

And, of course, I thank my patient husband Harry Ezratty, for putting up with my constant chatter about and references to food, chefs, restaurants, recipes and ingredients, even as I sometimes serve a lone baked potato for dinner.

Introduction

By Lars Rusin, Founder
Baltimore Foodies, Inc.
www.baltfoodies.com

One of the great things about life is that we never know exactly what's around the corner. It's all a game of chance.

Prior to my relocation in 1993, I'd never been to Baltimore. To me, one of the best ways to explore and learn a new place is to experience its great restaurants, and Charm City did not disappoint. I fell in love with the city, but even I wouldn't have imagined that in the space of a decade I would become a Baltimore Foodie.

In recent history, we've had the Baby Boomers, Yuppies, and Generation X. There's also a group of food lovers out there I like to call the Food TV Generation. Thanks to their devotion to the food cable channel and to a multitude of culinary blogs, magazines, books, and clubs, the culinary scene in Baltimore – and throughout the United States – has exploded over the past dozen years.

People now want to meet the chefs and learn not only where they studied, but where they shop and how they prepare a certain dish. It has become a status symbol to walk into a restaurant and know the chef.

Baltimore is home to many great chefs doing some incredible work, and you'll find many of them in these pages. Some were born here; others followed a culinary path to the city; a few started here, left, and returned. We have chefs who work for someone else and chefs who run their own establishments. Their training may have been at the front of the house or as dishwashers or at culinary school, either overseas or right here in Baltimore.

In the big picture, the chefs' pedigrees or resumes don't really matter. What matters is that these great chefs of Baltimore are sharing their recipes with you. By doing so, they are sharing the love they have for their profession, for their craft, and for Baltimore.

Read on and enjoy. Try some, or all, of the recipes. Most importantly, get out and meet some of the chefs who contributed to this volume. That way, the next time you go a restaurant you'll be able to say you know the chef.

Enjoy,
~LARS~

Terms and Methods

Bain Marie is a French term, which describes a half-filled pan of water heated in the oven into which a container of food is placed to cook. If this method of cooking is used on top of the stove, it's called a double boiler.

Brûlée is another French term for sprinkling sugar on top of (usually) a pudding and letting it caramelize by either direct flame (professionals use a kitchen torch) or under the broiler of your oven.

Demi-glace is a brown stock made of veal and tomato puree, thickened with a brown roux. A roux is a cooked mixture of equal parts flour and fat (butter, oil or bacon fat). It gets very thick as it cooks, and the longer it cooks, the darker it becomes.

To **deglaze** a pan is to use a small amount of liquid (wine is wonderful; you can use water or stock instead) to stir up the residue clinging to the bottom of the pan after you remove the items that have been cooking. These bits are highly concentrated in flavor, and the addition of liquid turns it into a tasty sauce or gravy base.

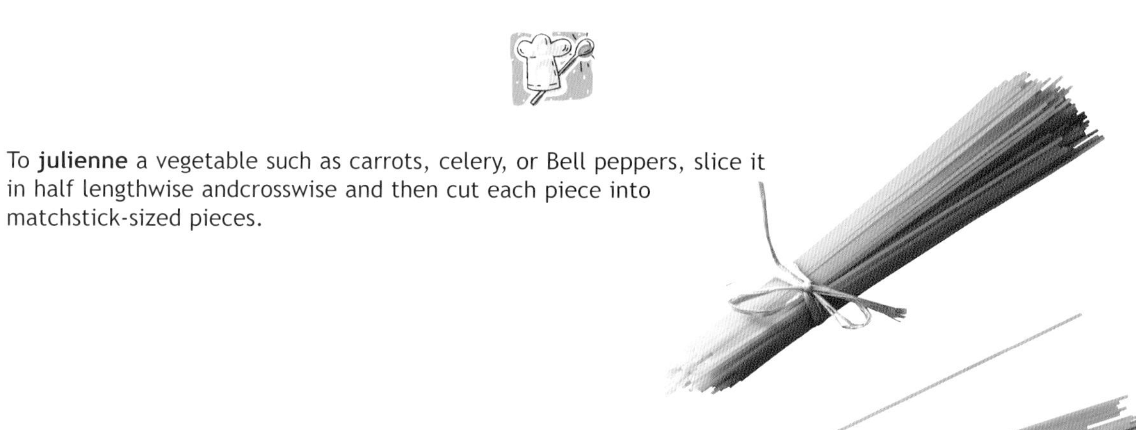

To **julienne** a vegetable such as carrots, celery, or Bell peppers, slice it in half lengthwise andcrosswise and then cut each piece into matchstick-sized pieces.

Cooking Tips

Rice will be fluffier and whiter if you add one teaspoon of lemon juice to each quart of water.

To keep an onion-half fresh in the refrigerator for a longer time, rub the leftover side with butter and it will keep fresh longer.

Store whole lemons in a tightly sealed jar of water in the refrigerator. They will yield much more juice than when first purchased.

Sunlight doesn't ripen tomatoes; warmth does.

Fresh parsley may be frozen.

Chill cheese before grating and it will grate faster.

If you scald tomatoes to make it easier to peel them, be sure to have them in the hot water for only a few seconds and then dip them immediately into ice water (to prevent them from cooking).

To remove fat from soup, refrigerate until the fat hardens on the top of the pot. Then you can just scoop it out.

To tenderize steak, rub in a mixture of cooking vinegar and oil and let it stand in the refrigerator for two hours.

Chop garlic with a small amount of salt, to prevent pieces from sticking to the knife or chopping board.

Save the juice from canned tomatoes in ice cube trays. When frozen, store in plastic bags in the freezer for cooking use or tomato drinks.

Egg whites can be kept up to one year. Add them to a plastic container as you collect them for use in meringues, angel food cake, etc. One cup equals seven or eight egg whites. You can also refreeze defrosted egg whites.

To keep fish from sticking to a baking plan, bake on a bed of chopped onion, celery and parsley. This also adds a nice flavor to the fish.

To rid cutting boards of onion, garlic or fish smell, cut a lime in two and rub the surface with the cut side of the fruit.

To prevent the bottom of the cake from sticking to the plate, sprinkle your serving plate with sugar before you place a cake on it.

Photo: Laura Magruder

Great Chefs of **BALTIMORE**

Contents

Appetizers, Soups and Salads

Great Chefs of **BALTIMORE**

Contents

Pasta & Veggies

Meats: Beef, Veal & Pork

Great Chefs of BALTIMORE

Contents

Poultry

Seafood

Contents

Seafood

Great Chefs of **BALTIMORE**

Contents

Desserts

To avoid last minute surprises, read the entire recipe before you begin.

Photo: Annie Reid-Stone

Appetizers, Soups and Salads

The recipes in this section will get you through all types of gatherings. Delicious hot and cold appetizers, soups, and salads are by some of Baltimore's most admired chefs; their names and restaurants appear before each recipe.

Chef	Restaurant	Location
Marc Attman	Attman's Delicatessen	Corned Beef Row
Nick Bates	The Bicycle	Federal Hill
Robert Cernak	Obrycki's	Fell's Point
John Creger	Gibby's Seafood	Lutherville
Donna Crivello	Donna's Cafes & Coffee Bars	City-wide
Rashed Edwards	Kali's Court	Fell's Point
Eric Huckleberry	Ryan's Daughter	Belvedere Square
Christopher Lewis	The Brass Elephant	Mt. Vernon
Brian Martin	Kali's Court	Fell's Point
Kevin Miller	IXIA	Mt. Vernon
Felix Nuñez	Window's at Renaissance Harborplace	Inner Harbor
Barry Rumsey	Formerly of The Bicycle	Federal Hill
Emilio Sanz	Tío Pepe Restaurant	Mt. Vernon
John Shields	Gertrude's	Wyman Park
Jeffrey Smith	The Chameleon Café	Lauraville
Bryan Sullivan	Formerly of Bistro 888	Fells Point
Sonny Sweetman	Abacrombie Fine Foods	Cultural District
Franklin Thomas	George's, Peabody Court Hotel	Mt. Vernon
Frances Thompson	George's, Peabody Court Hotel	Mt. Vernon
Graham Weber	Formerly of Grill 700	Harbor East
William Wesner	Blue Sea Grill	Downtown
Eric Yeager	Baldwin's Station	Sykesville

Photo: Annie Reid-Stone

Attman's Delicatessen
Chef Marc Attman

Attman's Reuben Dip

Serves a crowd

2 lbs.	corned beef, chopped
1 lb.	shredded Swiss cheese
1/2 cup	ketchup
4 TB.	mustard
1/2 cup	chopped yellow onions
1/2 cup	sweet pickle relish
1 lb.	cream cheese, at room temperature
1 cup	sour cream
1	12-inch round Russian rye bread (for serving bowl)
1	loaf rye bread, cubed, for dipping

❶To make the dip, combine the corned beef, Swiss cheese, ketchup, mustard, onions, relish, cream cheese and sour cream in a large bowl.

❷Stir until ingredients are well blended.

❸Cut the top off the round Russian rye bread; scoop out the insides. Add the dip to the hallowed-out bread and refrigerate until ready to serve.

❹Use cubes of rye bread to dip – or halved celery stalks.

Photo: Annie Reid-Stone

The Bicycle
CHEF NICK BATES

Spicy Corn and Crab Soup

Serves 6 to 8

1/4 cup	vegetable oil
1/2 cup	diced carrots
1/2 cup	diced celery
1 cup	diced onions
4 TB.	chopped garlic
1 cup	white wine
2	bay leaves
2 TB.	fresh thyme
2 qt.	vegetable stock
1 cup	sweet chili sauce
1 tsp.	ground cumin
2	*poblano* peppers, roasted
1 tsp.	ground *chipotle* pepper
1 tsp.	cayenne pepper
1 tsp.	onion powder
2 TB.	dry oregano
1 TB.	celery salt
2 lbs.	frozen yellow corn
1 cup	heavy cream
1 lb.	Maryland Blue Crab claw meat
✓	Salt and Pepper to taste

❶ Heat oil over medium flame.

❷ Sweat onions, celery, and carrots until tender and aromatic, then add garlic and sauté for additional 5 minutes.

❸ Deglaze with white wine, add bay leaves and fresh thyme, then reduce by half.

❹ Add vegetable stock, chili sauce, cumin, peppers, onion powder, oregano and celery salt and bring to a simmer for 15 minutes.

❺ Add corn and bring back to a simmer, then add heavy cream and puree soup.

❻ Strain soup if desired, and then add crab meat.

❼ Taste, to see if more salt and pepper is needed.

Photo courtesy of Obrycki's

Obrycki's
Chef Robert Cernak

Obrycki's Crab Dip

Serves a crowd

1 lb.	back fin crab meat
1 lb.	cream cheese, softened
1/3 cup	sour cream
2 TB.	mayonnaise
2 TB.	hot sauce
2 TB.	Worcestershire sauce
1	egg
2/3 cup	fresh breadcrumbs
1 TB.	diced onion
2 TB.	red seafood seasoning (e.g. Old Bay)
✓	pinch salt and white pepper
3 oz.	shredded cheddar cheese (reserve 1 ounce for topping)
✓	Bread or crackers to use as dippers.

❶Preheat oven to 350°.

❷Pick through crabmeat, removing any shell, without breaking up the lumps of crabmeat. Set aside.

❸Blend all the other ingredients well. Then fold the crabmeat into other ingredients.

❹Place the dip into a greased casserole dish, smooth to an even depth. Top with reserved cheddar cheese.

❺Bake until the cheese on top is melted and the dip is hot throughout. Time varies according to individual ovens and pan sizes.

❻Serve with bread, crackers or the dipper of your choice.

Gibby's Seafood

CHEF JOHN CREGER

Amaretto Shrimp

Serves 4

12	large shrimp peeled and deveined
1 TB.	clarified butter*
1/4 cup	Amaretto
1/2 cup	chicken stock
✓	butter

❶In a large saucepan, cook shrimp in clarified butter until almost done. Remove shrimp to plate; drain pan.

❷Deglaze** with Amaretto, reducing until almost half.

❸Add shrimp to pan; add chicken stock to pan slowly, reducing until almost 1/4 is left. Finish with butter. (More or less butter can be added, to achieve the quantity you need.)

❹To serve, place shrimp on serving plate; drizzle with sauce. Enjoy!

* *To clarify butter, let it melt in pan slowly and skim off the foam that accumulates. The clear golden color that's left is clarified butter.*

** *To deglaze a pan, pour off fat. Add stock or wine, in this case, Amaretto. Turn up heat and stir to get up all the bits stuck to the bottom of the pan. Some will melt, making a flavor-rich base for cooking.*

This is a pleasantly sweet sauce. It goes great with toasted French bread. It can even go over some pasta, for a light starter.

Gibby's Seafood
CHEF JOHN CREGER

Tempura Scallops

Serves 2-5

✓	Oil for frying
10	sea scallops, fresh
1/4 cup	cornstarch for dredging
1/2 cup	cornstarch for batter
1	can beer (or less)
2 TB.	soy sauce
✓	wooden skewers
✓	ginger for dipping
✓	garlic for dipping
✓	soy sauce for dipping
✓	lemon or lime juice

❶Preheat oil in deep fryer.

❷Dredge scallops lightly in dry cornstarch.

❸Mix together enough cornstarch, beer and soy sauce to form a batter.

❹Dip the dusted scallops in batter to coat.

❺Put the scallops on the end of a skewer to hold, when first going into the oil. This helps to prevent sticking and keeps the batter on.

❻Serve with various dipping sauces, made of mixtures of soy sauce flavored with either ginger, garlic, lemon or lime juice.

I recommend serving these on a bed of thinly sliced leeks, sautéed lightly in sesame oil.

Photo: Annie Reid-Stone

Donna's Cafes & Coffee Bars

CHEF DONNA CRIVELLO

Donna's Minestrone

3 or 4 TB.	olive oil
1	small yellow onion, diced
1 stalk	celery, diced
1/2 cup	chopped fresh fennel (optional)
1 or 2	carrots, diced
4 to 5	cloves garlic, chopped
1/2 cup	wine (optional)
2 to 3 qts.	cold water (to cover all vegetables by 1 inch)
1	leek, washed and diced
1/2 head	cabbage, chopped
6	fresh plum tomatoes, chopped
1	small zucchini, washed and chopped
1/2 cup	green beans or peas
14 ozs.	diced tomatoes (one can)
2	bay leaves and fresh herbs (parsley, thyme, oregano)
1 cup	cannellini beans or garbanzo beans (soaked overnight, then cooked) (or use canned)
1 cup	cooked pasta or rice (optional)
✓	salt & pepper
✓	grated Parmesan or Romano cheese

Serves 8-10

A basic vegetable soup; use leftovers as "ribolitta," cooked again the next day.

❶ Heat oil in bottom of large heavy stock pot. Add chopped onions, then celery, carrots, (fennel if used) and garlic. Add a little salt when sautéing vegetables.

❷ When vegetables begin to soften, add wine, water (or stock) to cover, and simmer about 10 to 15 minutes.

❸ Add the rest of the vegetables, bay leaves and fresh herbs. Simmer for about 1 hour.

❹ Add cooked or canned beans and continue to cook for another half hour then add cooked pasta if desired.

❺ Taste and add salt and pepper.

❻ Serve in individual bowls topped with grated cheese; refrigerate any leftovers.

For *ribolitta* (recooked soup)

8 to 10	slices of day old or toasted rustic bread

❶ Bring leftovers slowly to a boil, and then simmer.

❷ Arrange toasted bread on the bottom of bowls and ladle hot soup on top.

❸ Top with grated cheese and serve.

Photo: Annie Reid-Stone

Donna's Cafes & Coffee Bars
CHEF DONNA CRIVELLO

Donna's Roasted Vegetable Salad

Serves 6-8

1	small eggplant, sliced in 3/4 inch rounds and set on towels to dry* for 30 minutes
✓	olive oil
✓	salt and pepper
1 or 2	red Bell peppers, cut in half, seeds out
12	red potatoes, washed and cut into wedges
4	large sweet potatoes, cut into 2-inch cubes
✓	fresh rosemary
1/2 head	cauliflower, broken into large florets
2	carrots, peeled, sliced on the diagonal 1/4 inch thick
2	beets, washed and sliced, 1/4 inch thick
1 can	artichoke hearts, drained (or 6 minis, blanched)
1	medium red onion, sliced in 1/2 inch rounds
✓	fresh thyme

❶Preheat oven to 375°. Have ready sturdy baking sheets and a pastry brush.

❷**Eggplant**: Brush the bottom of baking sheet with a thin layer of olive oil. Place dried* eggplant on baking sheet; brush tops with oil. Season with salt and pepper. Roast until golden and tender, approximately 20 minutes.

❸**Red peppers:** Cover the bottom of baking sheet with aluminum foil, then thin layer of olive oil (or pan spray). Place peppers cut side down. Roast 20-25 minutes until tops have blistered and the flesh is tender but still a little firm (do not overcook). Wrap the peppers in the foil to help "steam off" the skins. When cooled, peel off skins.

❹**Potatoes:** (red and sweet can be combined on same sheet): Brush pan with olive oil, and top of potatoes with olive oil, salt and pepper and fresh rosemary. Roast until browned and tender (approximately 35-40 minutes). Taste to check for doneness.

❺Cauliflower, carrots, beets, artichokes and onions can be combined on same sheets (space permitting). Brush pan with olive oil, then tops of vegetables. Season with salt and pepper and fresh thyme. Roast until browned and tender (approximately 25 minutes; to check doneness, pierce with fork and taste).

❻All vegetables can be served together at room temperature, artfully arranged on a platter with mixed greens, tossed with balsamic vinaigrette (recipe follows on next page) and finished with shaved Pecorino or grated Romano cheese.

Continued...

This is an original salad that's been on our menu for over 10 years. Vegetables are roasted each day, placed atop mixed greens and dressed with our own balsamic vinaigrette.

Donna's Cafes & Coffee Bars

CHEF DONNA CRIVELLO

Donna's Roasted Vegetable Salad (continued)

Balsamic Vinaigrette Salad Dressing

Serves 6-8

1/3 cup	Balsamic vinegar
1 tsp.	Dijon mustard
1	large clove garlic, chopped
2/3 cup	pure or extra virgin olive oil
✓	salt and pepper
1-2 cups	dry greens**

❶Measure 1/3 cup vinegar in a jar. Add Dijon mustard and chopped garlic.

❷Whisk in olive oil (as you are whisking the oil, you are creating an emulsion*

❸Add a little more oil if you wish, still whisking. Also, add salt and freshly ground pepper to taste.

❹Keep in refrigerator; bring to room temperature before using. You may need to shake or whisk.

❺In a large bowl, using 1 to 2 cups of dry greens**, drizzle on about 1/3 cup of vinaigrette (be sure it is emulsified or mixed).

* ***Emulsion**: the binding of two liquids, slowing adding one liquid while rapidly mixing, disperses and suspends minute droplets of one liquid throughout the other, ending up with a satiny smooth mixture. Mustard helps to bind the oil and vinegar.*

** ***Bagged greens** are pre-washed, but if you are using arugula, spinach or another very sandy green, they must be thoroughly washed free of grit. Method: fill large bowl with cold water, submerge greens, lift and drain in colander. Rinse sand from bowl. Refill with water; repeat washing until greens are grit-free.*

Ryan's Daughter
CHEF ERIC HUCKLEBERRY

Cream O'Broccoli Soup with Dubliner Cheese

Serves a crowd

Roux:

1 lb.	Kerrygold butter (available at Great Cheese Company)
1 lb.	all purpose flour

Soup:

3 TB.	olive oil
1	yellow onion, diced small
1 TB.	minced garlic
5 bunches	fresh broccoli, cut in a small dice and using 1/4 of the stem
3 pints	chicken stock (you can use bouillon cubes, chicken base or canned stock)
1 pint	heavy whipping cream
1 1/2 lbs.	Kerrygold Dubliner cheese, shredded
✓	salt and pepper to taste

❶ **Roux**: Melt the butter in a pot on low heat; add the flour and mix for 7 minutes over medium-low heat. Put to the side and reserve.

❷ **Soup**: Place olive oil, onion, garlic, and broccoli in a stock pot and sauté for 10 minutes over a medium heat, stirring constantly so it doesn't burn, until the onions are translucent.

❸ Add the stock and heavy cream, put on high heat and bring to a boil.

❹ Reduce liquid by a third. While the soup is boiling, add half of the roux and put on medium flame, stirring constantly for 10 minutes until the roux cooks out. The soup should have a medium consistency. If not, add the rest of the roux and re-thicken.

❺ Add the Dubliner cheese and keep stirring until the cheese melts completely. The soup should coat the back of a spoon.

❻ Season with salt and pepper to taste. Serve and enjoy!

Dubliner cheese makes this basic cream soup come to life! Dubliner cheese is imported from Ireland by the Great Cheese Company in Baltimore.

Photo: Annie Reid-Stone

The Brass Elephant
Chef Christopher Lewis

Seafood Ceviche

Serves a crowd

2 lbs.	scallops and squid
2 TB.	pink peppercorns
2 TB.	lemon juice
2 TB.	orange juice
1/4 cup	oil
2 tsp.	salt
1 tsp.	pepper
1/2 tsp.	chopped chives

❶ Dice the seafood.

❷ Mix other ceviche ingredients together and then add diced seafood.

❸ Let marinate in refrigerator for one hour.

❹ Serve as a cold appetizer, or use as garnish for Brass Elephant Gazpacho (recipe below).

Brass Elephant Gazpacho

Serves a crowd

5	tomatoes, peeled and seeded
1	roasted red pepper
5	cucumbers, peeled & seeded
1	green pepper
1	bunch scallions
1/2	red onion
1	clove garlic
1 gallon	tomato juice
1/2 cup	red wine vinegar
1/4 cup	extra virgin olive oil
1 TB.	cumin
1/2 TB.	white pepper
2 TB.	salt
5 dashes	Tabasco
1/2 cup	Tequila (burned off)

❶ Dip tomato into boiling water for a few seconds; then dip into ice water. Peel will come right off.

❷ Roast red pepper over grill or flame or in oven until skin blackens. It will then peel off.

❸ Rough chop other vegetables.

❹ Puree all vegetables in blender, but don't liquefy; there should be some pieces in it. Season with remaining ingredients.

❺ Add Tequila and carefully ignite. Let burn until flame goes out.

❻ Chill. Can be served as is, or garnished with Brass Elephant Seafood Ceviche (above).

Photo: Scott T. Mislan

Kali's Court

CHEFS BRIAN MARTIN & RASHED EDWARDS

Roasted Acorn Squash Bisque

with Chestnuts, Dried Cranberries, and Butternut Squash Chips

Serves 6 to 8

2	acorn squash, large
5 TB.	butter
2 TB.	light brown sugar
3 TB.	Kosher salt
4 tsp.	ground cinnamon
1/2	small white onion, diced
2 1/2 cups	light chicken stock
2 cups	heavy cream
4	chestnuts, roasted and shaved thin
18	re-hydrated dried cranberries
1	small butternut squash
✓	oil for frying

❶ Preheat oven to 400°.

❷ Cut two large acorn squash in halves, remove seeds and save.

❸ Spread halves cut side up on pan; sprinkle with sugar, cinnamon and salt. Divide four tablespoons butter into squash cups and roast in oven for 30 to 40 minutes, until tender.

❹ In a sauce pot, melt remaining butter and sweat the onion and acorn squash seeds until onion is soft. Add stock and cream. Simmer 3 minutes.

❺ Strain stock and scoop flesh from squash. Combine and blend until smooth, then strain.

❻ Peel and shave butternut squash into strips, using a vegetable peeler.

❼ To finish: Fry squash chips in oil until crisp. Ladle soup into bowls, divide chestnuts and cranberries into bowls and garnish with chips.

Photo: Annie Reid-Stone

IXIA

CHEF KEVIN MILLER

Tuna Tartar with Coconut Milk, Citrus, and Red Chilies

Serves 4

1	green plantain
2 cups	oil for frying
✓	salt, to taste
½ lb.	sushi quality tuna
2	ripe avocados, diced

Vinaigrette:

2 tsp.	fresh grated ginger
1	shallot, minced
✓	zest and juice of 1 lime
✓	zest and juice of 1 orange
3 TB.	rice vinegar
1 tsp.	Thai fish sauce*
1 TB.	honey
1	Thai red chili, seeded and finely minced
1 TB.	chopped fresh cilantro
½ cup	canned coconut milk
1 TB.	oil
1 tsp.	toasted sesame oil

❶ Peel and thinly slice plantain.

❷ Heat 2 cups fry oil in shallow pan to 350° and fry plantain chips until lightly browned and crispy, about 1 minute. Drain on paper towels and season with salt.

❸ Dice tuna and place in stainless steel bowl; store over another bowl of crushed ice; cover with plastic wrap and refrigerate.

❹ **Vinaigrette:** in a separate bowl add minced ginger and shallot, citrus juices and zest, rice vinegar, Thai fish sauce, honey, red chili and cilantro. Whisk in coconut milk and oils (this will keep in a sealed jar for one week in the refrigerator).

❺ To Serve: In a separate bowl, add diced tuna and avocado. Gently stir in vinaigrette with a spoon and serve in a chilled bowl. This will make 4 servings. Garnish with a couple of plantain chips and a sprig of cilantro.

* *Thai fish sauce or Nam Pla can be found in any Asian market.*

Great Chefs of BALTIMORE

Window's Restaurant, Renaissance Harborplace Hotel

CHEF FELIX NUÑEZ

Smoked Salmon and Crab Terrine

with Roasted Tomatoes, Spinach and Chive Oil

Serves 12

1 lb.	Maryland jumbo lump crab meat
3 TB.	mayonnaise
1/4 cup	scallions, finely diced
1 tsp.	soy sauce
1 tsp.	Worcestershire sauce
1 lb.	smoked salmon slices
2 lbs.	baby spinach, blanched, cooled & drained
✓	Oven roasted tomatoes (recipe below)
✓	Balsamic vinegar, 8 years or older
✓	Chive oil (recipe below)

Oven roasted tomatoes:

20	Roma tomatoes
1 cup	extra virgin olive oil
✓	freshly ground black pepper
✓	fresh oregano, thyme, basil, garlic, chopped

Chive Oil:

1	bunch chives
1 cup	salad oil
✓	salt and freshly ground pepper

❶ For terrine, pick through crab meat and remove all shells. In a mixing bowl, stir mayonnaise, scallions, soy sauce, and Worchester sauce. Fold in the crab meat. Refrigerate for 20 minutes.

❷ Line a large mold with plastic wrap. Lay in one layer of smoked salmon. Over that, fill mold one-third up with crab mixture. Add a layer of spinach and another layer of oven-dried tomatoes. Top with rest of crab meat mixture. Seal top with smoked salmon. Wrap whole terrine with plastic wrap and refrigerate. Use within 48 hours.

❸ For oven roasted tomatoes, cut Roma tomatoes in quarters and toss with oil, pepper, oregano, thyme, basil and garlic. Place in roasting pan and slow roast at 180° oven for 6 to 8 hours. (Or, you can use the jars of roasted tomatoes. Pat them dry to use in terrine.)

❹ For chive oil, use one bunch of chives. Add salad oil, salt to taste and freshly ground pepper.

❺ To plate, drizzle chive oil and Balsamic vinegar in a crisscross design on the plate. Slice one inch from the terrine mold. Place the slice on the left of the plate, standing upright. Place two roasted tomatoes to the right of the terrine. Top the terrine with baby spinach that has been mixed with a little chive oil.

Sea Scallops in Beggar's Purse

Serves a crowd

Scallop Marinade

3 lbs.	fresh sea scallops, halved
1 TB.	hot sauce (your favorite)
16 oz.	mango juice
1 cup	mixed herbs: chervil, dill, tarragon & oregano
1	red onion, fine diced
4 TB.	lime juice
✓	salt and pepper to taste

Beggar's Purse

2 bunches	scallions (blanched)
2 pkgs.	Goat cheese
1 cup	mixed herb blend
1 cup	melted butter
1 bag	baby spinach leaves
2 pkgs.	Feuille de brick
3	marinated scallops
1 cup	white & black sesame seeds with mustard seeds (equal parts of each)

❶Combine ingredients for marinade and marinate scallops overnight in this mixture; assemble next day.

❷Scallions need to be blanched in boiling, salted water for 30 seconds to be pliable enough to gather pastry and tie into a knot to make the purses. Separate scallion ribs, so they are ready to use.

❸Form Goat cheese disks by making a cherry tomato-size ball in your hands and gently pressing ball to form a silver dollar size cheese disk; sprinkle with herb blend. Make 20 of these.

❹Preheat oven to 350° and prepare for assembly with the following: (a) melted butter in cup ready with pastry brush, (b) spinach leaves in a large bowl, (c) baking sheet coated with vegetable spray, (d) Feuille de Brick unwrapped and ready.

❺Drain the marinated scallops and reserve juice (we don't want scallops to be juicy).

❻Brush sheet of pastry lightly with butter. Peel off of paper and flip over (we do this because when building ingredients, it's difficult to peel back pastry).

❼Put small handful of spinach in center of Feuille de Brick. Place small handful of scallops on top of spinach. Place goat's cheese disk on top of scallops. Sprinkle with seed blend and place on baking sheet (careful not to touch one to the other).

❽Bake 15 minutes or until golden brown.

❾Serve with beurre blanc or your favorite sauce.

This recipe is a popular, signature appetizer: Tender marinated scallops, goat's cheese and spinach wrapped inside of delicate French pastry dough called Feuille de Brick. The Feuille de Brick is paper thin, similar to Greek phyllo dough.It may be found in finer gourmet markets. A large crepe can substitute for the Feuille de Brick.

Photo: Annie Reid-Stone

Tío Pepe Restaurant
Chef Emilio Sanz

Tío Pepe's Sangria

Serves 2 or more

1/3 cup	sliced apple
1/3 cup	sliced orange
1/3 cup	sliced lemon
✓	ice cubes
2 TB.	sugar
3 oz.	Triple Sec
3 oz.	brandy
1	large bottle heavy red table wine
✓	club soda

❶ Place sliced fruit in a 1 1/2 quart or 2 quart pitcher and fill with ice cubes. Add sugar, Triple Sec and brandy.

❷ Stir with a wooden spoon and pour in wine to fill pitcher.

❸ Work spoon up and down hard enough to crush fruit and mix thoroughly.

❹ Add a dash of club soda after mixing to give sparkle.

❺ Adjust sugar to taste.

This recipe for Spanish style Sangria makes a lovely accompaniment for a romantic dinner. Another good choice for a romantic evening is a red Pesquera.

Great Chefs of **BALTIMORE**

Gertrude's

CHEF JOHN SHIELDS

Tangier Island Sea Clam Chowder

Serves 4 or more

4 TB.	bacon fat
2	onions, finely diced
4	large potatoes, peeled and cubed
4 cups	chopped clams, fresh, frozen, or canned with juice reserved
✓	salt & freshly ground black pepper
✓	Dough Boys (recipe next page)

❶Heat the bacon fat in a pot over medium heat and sauté the onions until tender.

❷Add the potatoes and the reserved clam juice. Add enough water to just barely cover the potatoes. Cook uncovered about 30 minutes or until potatoes can be pierced with a knife.

❸Add the chopped clams and if necessary, a bit more clam juice or water to just cover the potato-clam mixture. Reduce heat and simmer for 20 minutes more, or until clams are tender.

❹Season to taste with salt and pepper. Let the chowder rest for at least 30 minutes before serving.

❺When ready to serve, place the chowder back on the stove and return to medium heat. When mixture is quite hot, place the dough boys on top of the bubbling chowder. Place a lid on the pot and continue to simmer for 15 minutes, or until dough boys have become dupling-esque. Serve in bowls with plenty of bread.

Smith Island, Virginia is a remote outpost in the middle of the Chesapeake Bay; not far from where the Bay merges with the Atlantic Ocean. It's not a place for the faint of heart for the elements can at times be quite unforgiving. When the cold winds of winter blow, one understands why chowders were originally created - they warm you through and through. This chowder, which I serve often as a special at Gertrude's, is a version of one I learned from Alva Crockett, the five-time mayor of Tangier, and the great, great, grandson of Davy Crocket. Alva always used the large sea clams, shucking them and reserving their briny liquor. There is no flour used to thicken the soup - only potatoes and Alva's "dough boys." Another ingredient that may appear to be missing is the milk. Alva scolds, "milk is for babies and cereal, not for chowders." The man's right.

Gertrude's
CHEF JOHN SHIELDS

Tangier Island Sea Clam Chowder (continued)

Alva's Dough Boys

Serves 6-12

2 cups	flour
4 tsp.	baking powder
1 tsp.	salt
4 TB.	solid shortening (or lard)
1/2 cup	milk
1/2 cup	water

❶Sift together the flour, baking powder and salt into large bowl.

❷Work in the shortening with your fingertips or a pastry blender until the mixture is the consistency of coarse meal.

❸Combine the water and the milk and beat into the flour until a stiff (not wet) dough is formed.

❹Turn out the dough onto a lightly floured surface and knead gently for 1 minute. Return to bowl and cover with a towel until ready to use.

❺To form the "dough boys," pull pieces off the ball of dough about silver-dollar size and roll in the palms of your hands to form rounded balls. Place the pieces on a lightly floured platter and cover with a towel until ready to use.

❻This recipe makes a quite respectable biscuit and will yield about one dozen.

Dough Boys are cooked with soups and chowders - see preceeding recipe for the chef's recommended use.

Photo: Annie Reid-Stone

The Chameleon Café

CHEF JEFFREY SMITH

Grilled Lettuces

Serves 4

Dressing

1/4 cup	white wine vinegar
1/2 cup	heavy cream
3 cloves	garlic, minced
1 TB.	chopped fresh herbs
1/4 cup	extra virgin olive oil
1/2 tsp.	salt
1/2 tsp.	pepper

Salad

1 head	Romaine lettuce, quartered
1 head	red leaf lettuce, quartered
1 head	endive, quartered
2	carrots, peeled and cut into thin slices
8	green onions, bottoms removed
1 TB.	olive oil
1/4 cup	grated Parmesan cheese
✓	broken walnut meats (optional)

❶ Make dressing by mixing vinegar, cream, garlic and herbs together. Slowly mix in oil while constantly stirring. Season with salt and pepper.

❷ For the salad, lightly oil and season with salt and pepper the romaine, red leaf, endive, carrots and green onion.

❸ Place seasoned lettuces on a hot grill, turning constantly until wilted. Remove from grill.

❹ Ladle dressing on the salad and sprinkle Parmesan cheese on top. Sprinkle with walnuts, if desired, as pictured. Serve warm.

This is a very popular salad in our restaurant.

Photo: Tropical Dining archive

CHEF BRYAN SULLIVAN

Scallop & Crab Ceviche

Ceviche

1/2 lb.	jumbo lump crab
1/2 lb.	scallops (U-10 size)
1/3 cup	fresh lemon juice
1 bunch	chopped scallions
✓	pinch of sugar
✓	salt and pepper to taste

Blinis

1 cup	roasted corn cut off the cob
2 TB.	butter
1 TB.	chopped garlic
1/3 cup	cream
1	egg
1/4 cup	all-purpose flour
✓	pinch of baking soda
✓	salt and pepper to taste

Tomato Coulis

4	vine ripened tomatoes
2	cloves garlic, diced
2 oz.	olive oil
5	sprigs thyme
✓	salt and pepper to taste
✓	pinch of sugar

Serves 6 to 8

❶ For the Ceviche, pick the crab meat to remove all shells. Slice the scallops into quarters. Add lemon juice, scallions and season with sugar, salt and pepper. Let stand for 15 minutes.

❷ Sauté the fresh corn in butter; add the garlic. Once the corn is slightly brown, place mixture into a blender. Add the cream and mix until smooth.

❸ Place this mixture in a mixing bowl. Using a spatula, fold in the egg and flour mixed with baking soda. Season with salt, pepper and sugar to taste.

❹ Cook the batter (in circles of about one inch in diameter) just like pancakes, in a non-stick pan. [You can get the right amount by dropping batter from a quarter-cup measuring cup.]

❺ Preheat oven to 375° in preparing for the coulis.

❻ Cut tomatoes into quarters and arrange in a baking dish. Small-dice the garlic and rub onto each tomato. Drizzle olive oil onto the tomatoes.

❼ Remove thyme leaves from their stem and chop finely. Sprinkle thyme on the tomatoes and season with salt and pepper. Roast in 375° oven for 15 minutes.

❽ Remove from oven and place all ingredients in an electric blender, making sure to get all of the olive oil. Puree until smooth; adding a pinch of sugar to cut down some of the acidity.

❾ To serve, spoon the Tomato Coulis around the prepared Scallop and Crab Ceviche Blinis on the serving plate.

Photo: Annie Reid-Stone

Abacrombie Fine Foods & Accommodations

CHEF SONNY SWEETMAN

Smoked Red Pepper Flan

Serves 4

3	red peppers
2 cups	heavy cream
5	whole eggs
2 tsp.	paprika (smoked Spanish or Hungarian)
✓	salt and white pepper, to taste

❶ Preheat oven to 300º

❷ Roast peppers over an open flame until charred on the outside. Scrape off the charred pieces with a paring knife and remove the stem and seeds.

❸ Puree in a blender, with the remaining ingredients. Strain through a china cap.

❹ Pour one ounce of the mixture into glass ramekins and bake, covered with aluminum foil, in a bain marie* for 15 to 20 minutes or until soft but firm to the touch.

* *Bain Marie is the method of placing a baking pan into a larger baking pan that is half full of water.*

Photo: Annie Reid-Stone

George's, Peabody Court Hotel
CHEF FRANKLIN THOMAS

Duck Confit Springroll

with Blackberry Gastrique & Fig and Walnut Dressing

Makes 12

Blackberry Gastrique:

1/2 cup	sugar
2 pints	blackberries
1/2 cup	red wine vinegar
1 bottle	Zinfandel wine
2 tsp.	butter, softened

Fig and Walnut Dressing:

1/4 cup	olive oil
1/4 cup	lime juice
1/4 cup	chopped parsley
1 clove	garlic, minced
1/4 tsp.	salt
1/8 tsp.	pepper
1 cup	chopped walnuts
1 cup	fig puree

Spring Rolls:

3	8″ spring roll wrappers, quartered
1	leg duck confit, bone and skin removed, sliced thinly*
1 tsp.	minced shallots
1 oz.	red onion, julienne
1/4 cup	chopped arugula
1 tsp.	chopped thyme
1	grate of fresh black pepper
1 tsp.	Kosher salt
✓	fresh blackberries and orange segments for garnish

❶ For blackberry gastrique, carmelize the sugar in a heavy 2-quart saucepan over medium heat until golden brown.

❷ Add the blackberries, vinegar and Zinfandel. Reduce the mixture to only 2 cups.

❸ Strain through a fine mesh strainer and whisk in the soft butter. Keep sauce warm.

❹ For the dressing, combine oil, lime juice, parsley, garlic, salt, pepper and walnuts in a blender. Slowly incorporate the fig puree until all ingredients are blended well. Set aside.

❺ To assemble spring rolls, combine duck, shallots, onion, arugula and thyme. Place 1 tablespoon of mixture into each wrapper. Fold into spring roll shape. Seal with flour and water paste.

❻ Deep fry until golden brown. Serve warm.

❼ To Plate: Stripe one side of plate with the Gastrique and other with fig dressing. Place a small amount of greens in the center of the plate. Put the spring rolls on top of the greens and garnish with fresh blackberries and orange segments.

* *Duck confit is duck slowly cooked with herbs and garlic in duck fat. It is available prepackaged, in gourmet supermarkets.*

Photo: Annie Reid-Stone

George's, Peabody Court Hotel
CHEF FRANKLIN THOMAS

Mushroom Consommé
with Crispy Tofu, Black Truffles & Pine Nuts

Serves 10

Consommé

1½ lbs.	young fresh mushrooms
2	leeks
2 stalks	celery with leaves
2	medium carrots
4 cups	water
3 cans	vegetable consommé, heated
✓	salt and pepper to taste
½ cup	dry sherry

Crispy Tofu Squares

1 block	firm tofu, drained
2 TB.	toasted sesame oil
½ cup	sesame seeds
½ TB.	black pepper

To Plate

10 tsp.	Pine nuts
1 can	Black truffles (available in gourmet supermarkets)

❶Rinse mushroom, pat dry. Slice leeks down the center without cutting through; wash thoroughly. Rinse celery stalks and peel carrots. Chop all vegetables coarsely. Place in a saucepan and cover with water. Cover and simmer for 40 minutes, or until vegetables are cooked through.

❷Strain broth and discard vegetables. Stir broth into the hot vegetable consommé; season with salt and pepper. Lace consommé with sherry before serving.

❸**Tofu:** Place tofu between two cutting boards. Tip boards over sink edge and let excess liquid drain off for about 30 minutes. ❹Cube the pressed tofu into ¼- to ½- inch wide cubes. Place tofu cubes in bowl with sesame seeds and gently roll around to coat.

❺Heat remaining tablespoon of sesame oil in large non-stick skillet over medium heat. When hot, add seed-crusted tofu cubes and any remaining seeds. Cook, turning tofu cubes occasionally, until golden brown on both sides, about 5 to 7 minutes. Add the black pepper.

❻Toast the pine nuts in a 350° oven for 6 to 7 minutes, or until golden brown. Cool. Caution: pine nuts burn easily. Toasting will bring out the natural flavor.

❼**To Serve:** Pour equal amounts of hot consommé into 10 soup bowls; add 1 teaspoon pine nuts, tofu and 3 to 4 sliced black truffles. Serve immediately.

Photo: Annie Reid-Stone

George's, Peabody Court Hotel
CHEF FRANCES THOMPSON

Roasted Vidalia Onion Soup

Serves 6

2 lbs.	potatoes, quartered
3	Vidalia onions (medium), sliced thin
1/4 lb.	butter, divided
1 cup	flour
3 qts.	heavy cream
6 ozs.	chicken base
1	bay leaf
1 tsp.	black pepper
1/4 cup	white wine
✓	roux (recipe shown)

❶In a large pot, heat water and blanch the potatoes. Set aside.

❷While they are cooking, sauté the onions in half of the butter until they are almost translucent. Set aside.

❸To make roux, melt half of the butter in a sauté pan. Add 1 cup flour and whisk until they are mixed well.

❹In another large pot, add heavy cream, chicken base, bay leaf, black pepper and wine. Heat until cream is hot, then add the roux.

❺Reduce heat and let thicken.

❻Add reserved onion and potato and mix well. Serve hot.

Photo courtesy of Grill 700

CHEF GRAHAM WEBER

Grilled Oysters with Lime Butter

Serves 1

2 oz.	Lime tarragon compound butter (below)
6	Oysters on half shell
4 oz.	Rock salt
1	lime half, grilled

Lime Tarragon Butter

1 lb.	butter, cubed at room temperature
3	limes
1 bunch	tarragon, chopped

❶ To prepare Lime Butter, whip butter in a mixer until smooth and white.

❷ Zest limes and chop finely.

❸ Add zest to butter, then cut limes in half and juice into butter. Continue to whip until incorporated thoroughly.

❹ Remove butter from mixer and place in a bowl. Gently fold in tarragon.

❺ To prepare oysters, place one ounce of compound butter on each shucked oyster on half shell.

❻ Place oyster shell side down on grill until oyster is just cooked (approximately 3 minutes).

❼ Display 6 oyster half shells on a bed of rock salt and garnish with grilled lime.

This recipe does not call for salt or pepper because of the natural salt of the oyster and its delicate flavor need not compete with something as assertive as pepper.

Photo courtesy of Big Steak Management

Blue Sea Grill

Chef William Wesner

Ahi Tuna Tartar

Serves 2

4 oz.	Ahi Tuna, raw
1/2 oz.	Asian marinade (recipe follows)
2 oz.	seaweed salad
1 tsp.	Wasabi whipped cream (recipe follows)
1 tsp.	Tobiko (green)
3	Baguette chips (recipe follows)
2	shoots chives
1/4 tsp.	sesame seeds, black and white
1/4 tsp.	soy honey reduction (recipe follows)

Asian Marinade

2 TB.	aji marin
1 1/2 TB.	soy sauce
1/2 TB.	honey
1/2 TB.	lime juice
1 TB.	sesame oil
1/2 TB.	brown sugar
1 1/2 TB.	minced ginger
1	scallion
1 tsp.	red pepper flakes

Wasabi Whipped Cream

1/3 cup	crème fraiche
1 1/4 tsp.	Wasabi powder

Baguette Chips

1/4 loaf	baguette, cut 3/8" on bias
2 TB.	olive oil
2 TB.	Parmesan cheese

Soy Honey Reduction

1/3 cup	Aji Marin wine
1/3 cup	soy sauce
1/3 cup	honey

❶ To prepare Asian Marinade, combine all of its ingredients except scallions and pepper. Puree with burre mixer. Strain liquid. Add scallions and pepper flakes.

❷ To prepare Wasabi Whipped Cream, fold wasabi powder into crème fraiche.

❸ To prepare Baguette Chips, cut slices to crouton size. Lay out on a sheet pan. Drizzle with oil; sprinkle with cheese. Bake at 350° until toasted and crisp.

❹ To prepare Soy Honey Reduction, reduce marin and soy sauce over medium fire to 1/3 cup. Add honey to reduction; stir to blend.

❺ To assemble, place mound of seaweed off center of plate. Finely dice tuna; fold in Asian marinade.

❻ Place ring mold in center of plate; pack with tuna mixture, then remove ring. Add a dollop of whipped cream, top with green tobiko.

❼ Garnish plate with baguette chips and chives. Drizzle with soy honey reduction and sprinkle with sesame seeds.

Photo: Annie Reid-Stone

Baldwin's Station
CHEF ERIC YEAGER

Grilled Watermelon & Shrimp

Serves 4

8	limes (juiced), divided
4 TB.	sugar
8 oz.	extra virgin olive oil, divided
8 oz.	cilantro
12	shrimp (size16-20), peeled and deveined
4 slices	red watermelon (3 inches wide)
4 slices	yellow watermelon (3 inches wide)
4 oz.	rum
8	shallots, sliced fine
8 oz.	Tequila
1 oz.	butter

❶Mix together most of the lime juice, 3 tablespoons of sugar, most of the olive oil and cilantro until emulsified; pour over uncooked shrimp. Refrigerate for one hour.

❷Brush watermelon with the rum and place on the grill. Mark both sides; remove from heat.

❸Place shrimp on grill marking both sides, making sure you first drain off most of the marinade to reduce flame on the grill.

❹On stove, place shallots in a sauce pot with a little olive oil and sauté until translucent. Then add tequila and cook till alcohol burns off. Add the remaining lime juice, sugar and 1 oz. of butter. Strain; reserve sauce.

❺For 4 individual servings, place 2 slices of watermelon on each plate, criss-crossing each color. Place shrimp on top and garnish with sauce.

Just reading this recipe gets your mouth watering, doesn't it? Nice, light and perfect for a summer garden party. Preparation is quick and easy, so you can enjoy the party too. And as long as you have the rum and tequila handy, some tropical drinks would be a perfect compliment to this appetizer - don't forget the little umbrellas!

Photo: Annie Reid-Stone

Baldwin's Station
CHEF ERIC YEAGER

Poached Peach Soup with Champagne Granita

Serves 4

8	peaches
1 bottle	Riesling wine
1 cup	sugar
2 oz.	mint chiffonade (chopped)
1 qt.	heavy cream
✓	salt and pepper to taste
2 oz.	Peach Schnapps
1 split	Champagne
2 cups	simple syrup (heat equal parts sugar and water) or use Triple Sec
1 cup	crème frêche

❶ **For soup:** Wash peaches and place in sauce pan, cover with Riesling wine. If peaches are not submerged, add water to cover.

❷ Poach peaches until fork tender. Remove from pot; save liquid for later use.

❸ Skin the peaches, dice into small pieces and place in blender. Add Peach Schnapps.

❹ Puree peaches until smooth, adding some of the poaching liquid if not smooth (2 cups). Add sugar and mint to blender. While blending slowly, add heavy cream to desired consistency. Season with salt and pepper

❺ **For Garnish:** Mix champagne & simple syrup together, place in lipped sheet pan, place in freezer.

❻ **To serve:** In a bowl, add soup, shave frozen champagne granita over it, and add a dollop of crème freche.

Excellent choice if you are looking for a chilled summer soup that is delicate in flavor and pretty, too. Try serving in decorative stemware to enhance the presentation. Just as a visit to Baldwin's Station transports you to another time and place, so will this recipe.

Photos:
Annie Reid-Stone

Pasta & Veggies

The popularity of pasta in Baltimore probably began in our well-known Little Italy. And the number of Italian restaurants continues to grow. Both fine-dining and casual restaurants are devoted to pasta. Vegetarian meals are also easier to find, as many restaurants have added pasta and veggies to their menus.

Chef	Restaurant	Location
Assad Akbari	The Helmand Restaurant	Mt. Vernon
Nino Germano	La Scala Ristorante	Little Italy
Kevin Miller	IXIA	Mt. Vernon
Paul Oliver	Dalesio's of Little Italy	Little Italy
Michael Russell Jr.	Vespa	Federal Hill
Sonny Sweetman	Abacrombie Fine Foods	Cultural District
Cindy Wolf	Charleston	Fell's Point
Eric Yeager	Baldwin's Station	Sykesville

Photo courtesy of The Helmand Restaurant

The Helmand Restaurant
CHEF ASSAD AKBARI

Kaddo Bowrani
(Roasted Baby Pumpkin with Yogurt Sauce)

Serves 4-6

1	small pumpkin (baby or "spookies" work best)
1/4 cup	vegetable oil
1/4 cup	sugar
✓	cinnamon
✓	yogurt sauce (recipe follows)

❶Slice pumpkin and remove seeds. Peel outer skin. Slice into 2-inch pieces, lengthwise.

❷Preheat oven to 350°.

❸Place oil in skillet and heat to medium. Add pumpkin. Cook on medium heat, covered, for approximately 10 minutes, turning once.

❹Remove from pan and place in small roasting or baking pan. Sprinkle the pumpkin with the sugar and cinnamon. Cover tightly.

❺Bake at 350° for 30 minutes or until soft. Time may differ according to hardness of the pumpkin.

❻Serve warm with yogurt sauce.

Yogurt Sauce

1 cup	plain yogurt
1 tsp.	fresh garlic, diced
✓	dash salt

❶Stir until ingredients are smooth.

Photo: Annie Reid-Stone

La Scala Ristorante
CHEF NINO GERMANO

Portabella alla Griglia

Serves 2

✓	Portabella mushroom, cleaned
1	red Bell pepper, halved and cleaned
✓	olive oil
✓	fresh Mozarella cheese
✓	fresh basil, julienne
✓	salt and pepper to taste
✓	pinch dry oregano
1 oz.	extra virgin olive oil

❶Brush the mushroom and the red Bell pepper halves with olive oil and place on hot grill; roast on both sides.

❷To plate, slice mushroom and pepper, alternate with slices of mozzarella cheese.

❸Drizzle with extra virgin olive oil and sprinkle with the cut basil, dry oregano and salt and pepper to taste.

Photo: Annie Reid-Stone

IXIA

CHEF KEVIN MILLER

Roasted Sweet Potato Gnocchi

with Pure Maple Cream, Virginia Ham & Melted Greens

4	medium sweet potatoes
1 tsp.	Kosher salt
1/2 tsp.	ground white pepper
1/8 tsp.	fresh nutmeg
3/4 to 1	cup flour
1/4 cup	pure Vermont or Canadian Grade A Maple Syrup
3/4 cup	heavy cream
1/4 cup	diced Virginia Smithfield Ham
1 tsp.	salt
2 cups	fresh spinach
1 TB.	butter
1 TB,	olive oil
✓	salt and pepper to taste

Serves 6-8

❶Roast sweet potatoes in 350° oven until done (45 minutes to 1 hour).

❷Let cool for 1/2 hour.

❸Remove skin and place flesh in mixing bowl with salt, pepper and nutmeg. Mash by hand, with a whisk. Stir in flour with a wooden spoon until mixture forms a loose ball (dough will be slightly sticky).

❹Place on lightly floured board and knead by hand, working in more flour as necessary. Divide dough into four sections.

❺Working with one section at a time, roll into a long snake shape, about 1/2 inch in diameter. With a knife, cut into 1-inch pieces. Place on sheet pan and put in freezer.

❻In small sauce pan, add maple syrup, cream, and diced ham. Bring to a boil and reduce by half, or until slightly thickened.

❼In large 10 to 12 quart pasta pot, bring 8 quarts of water and 1 tsp. salt to a rolling boil. Boil gnocchi until they float to the surface, and continue to boil an additional minute (20 gnocchi maximum at one time). Remove gnocchi from water and drain.

❽Add gnocchi to sauce in pan and boil for 30 seconds.

❾Serve in warm bowl; sauté spinach with butter and olive oil. Season with salt and pepper. Garnish gnocchi with wilted spinach.

Dalesio's of Little Italy
CHEF PAUL OLIVER

Pennette con Rucolo e Salsiccia
Penette with Arugula & Sausage

Serves 6

1 TB.	unsalted butter
1 TB.	all-purpose flour
2 TB.	cooking oil
3	fresh sausages
1 1/2 lbs.	*Penette* Pasta
1 cup	water the pasta has cooked in
1	ripe tomato, peeled, seeded and cubed
✓	salt and pepper
4	bunches arugula
1 oz.	*Parmegiano Reggiano* cheese, grated

❶Work butter and flour together to make a *beurre manié*.*

❷Heat oil in saucepan; brown sausages on all sides; remove and slice.

❸Cook pasta in salted, boiling water. Drain, reserving one cup of cooking water for the sauce.

❹Add the diced tomato and reserved water to saucepan; add salt and pepper to taste as it cooks.

❺Return sausage slices to the pan and add arugula until it collapses.

❻Serve sausage, sauce and arugula over pasta.

* *Buerre manié is a kneaded butter used to thicken stews. Mix together the softened butter and flour with a fork. Add to the boiling water in small pieces; whisk together until butter melts and sauce thickens.*

Photo courtesy of Vespa

Vespa

CHEF MICHAEL RUSSELL JR.

Roasted Pepper Gnocchi with Tomatoes, Olives & Marjoram

Serves 4-6

1 lb.	Yukon Gold potatoes, peeled and cut
2	medium red Bell peppers, roasted, seeded, peeled and finely chopped
1	egg, beaten
1 tsp.	salt and pepper
1 cup	all purpose flour
4 TB.	olive oil
2	garlic cloves, thinly sliced
1 cup	Kalamata olives, pitted and diced
2 lbs.	ripe plum tomatoes, diced 1/2 inch
2 TB.	fresh marjoram

❶ In a large saucepan, boil the potatoes until tender, about 35 minutes.

❷ While still warm, pass the potatoes through a ricer.

❸ Place the peppers in a towel and ring out as much liquid as possible.

❹ Make a well in the center of the potatoes. Place egg, salt, and pepper in well. Stir together, and then add flour.

❺ Knead gently until a ball if formed, about four minutes.

❻ Divide dough into 4 balls. Roll one at a time into a 1-inch rope. Cut each rope into 1/2 inch pieces.

❼ Bring 4 quarts of water to a boil.

❽ Drop gnocchi into water and cook about 1 minute or until they float.

❾ Heat oil in skillet, add garlic and brown slightly. Add olives, tomatoes, and marjoram. Cook for about 3 minutes.

❿ Add gnocchi, toss and serve.

Photo: Annie Reid-Stone

Abacrombie Fine Foods & Accommodations

CHEF SONNY SWEETMAN

Truffle Scented Spaghetti Squash

Serves 2

1	spaghetti squash
✓	salt and pepper
1 TB.	white truffle oil
2 oz.	butter
2 sprigs	fresh thyme
1 cup	chicken stock, vegetable stock or water
✓	chopped chives for garnish

❶Preheat oven to 375°.

❷Cut the squash in half. Remove the seeds.

❸Season the inside of the squash with salt and pepper.

❹Place in a shallow baking dish and add the remaining ingredients (except the chives).

❺Bake for 15 or 20 minutes.

❻Allow to cool slightly so you can handle the squash.

❼Use a fork to scrape out the inside of the squash. It should resemble strands of spaghetti.

❽Place on serving dish and sprinkle with chopped chives for garnish.

Photo: Annie Reid-Stone

Charleston
CHEF CINDY WOLF

Fried Green Tomatoes with Chive Oil

Serves 4

2	unripe tomatoes
2 cups	cornmeal
1 tsp.	Kosher salt
1/2 tsp.	Cayenne pepper
✓	peanut oil for frying

❶ Slice washed tomatoes 1/4-inch thick.

❷ In a medium bowl, mix cornmeal, salt and cayenne. Dip tomato slices in cornmeal mixture, coating both sides. Lay coated slices on a cookie sheet.

❸ Prepare Chive Oil (recipe below).

❹ In a deep fryer or deep sauce pan, bring peanut oil to 350º.

❺ Gently slide tomato slices into hot oil. Fry until golden, about 40-60 seconds.

❻ Remove slices from oil with slotted spoon. Rest on paper towels to drain. Serve immediately, with Chive Oil.

Chive Oil

1 bunch	fresh chives
1/2 cup	olive oil
✓	salt to taste

❶ Combine one bunch of well-rinsed fresh chives with 1/2 cup olive oil. Place in blender and blend at highest speed for approximately 2 minutes or until smooth. Salt to taste.

❷ Shake well before serving. Drizzle on tomatoes, potatoes, or seafood.

Fried Green Tomatoes are a Southern tradition. The touch of spice and sweet cornmeal balance the acidity of the unripe tomato, and the quick frying softens the firm fruit just perfectly. The chive oil punctuates the flavors and adds a delicious splash of color.

Photo: Annie Reid-Stone

Baldwin's Station
Chef Eric Yeager

Fried Green Tomatoes with Crab Napolean

Serves 4

8 oz.	small diced potatoes
12	slices green tomato
2 cups	all-purpose flour
6	eggs
2 cups	Panko bread crumbs (Japanese bread crumbs)
1 oz.	olive oil
3 cups	heavy cream
8 oz.	crab claw meat
3 TB.	Old Bay seasoning
✓	salt and pepper to taste
8 oz.	Sherry
4 oz.	vegetable oil

❶Cook potatoes and drain. Set aside to cool.

❷Dredge the sliced tomatoes in flour, shake off any excess flour.

❸Whisk eggs.

❹Place the floured tomatoes into the whisked eggs and coat them. Then place tomatoes in the bread crumbs and completely coat them. Lay tomatoes on a sheet tray and refrigerate.

❺Heat olive oil in a pan. Sauté potatoes; add heavy cream and crab meat.

❻When cream starts to reduce, add the Old Bay seasoning, salt, pepper, and Sherry. Let reduce to a creamy consistency.

❼For the tomatoes, heat 4 ounces vegetable oil in a sauté pan. When hot, place the breaded tomato in the pan and cook until light golden brown. Remove. Repeat.

❽When plating, use a deep plate or shallow bowl to accommodate the sauce. Place one tomato at the bottom of each of 4 plates, then spoon potato and crab meat on top. Repeat this step one more time and top it off with a slice of fried tomato to form a tower.

❾Sprinkle a little Old Bay around the plate for garnish and ladle in the rest of the cream around the bottom of the plate.

Your guests will be delighted with this mini-architectural display, bursting with flavor and a sense of fun!

Photo: Tropical Dining archive

Meats

The chefs who bring us meat recipes are skilled in many forms of cooking, but a taste of their meat dishes will convince you that this is one of their specialties. Beef, pork, lamb, and veal are seared, baked, roasted, and stewed, with everything from asparagus, Maryland's Silver Queen corn, and plantains, to peaches, apricots, and exotic spices.

Chef	Restaurant	Location
Antonio Baines	Tapas Teatro	Station North
John "Tip" Carter IV	The Brewer's Art	Mt. Vernon
Mimmo Cricchio	Da Mimmo	Little Italy
Luis Diaz	Babalu Grill	Downtown
Russel Frew	Chiapparelli's Restaurant	Little Italy
Brian Hart	Shula's Steak House	Downtown
Christopher Lewis	The Brass Elephant	Mt. Vernon
Renato Rotondo, Sr.	Sabatino's Italian Restaurant	Little Italy
Graham Weber	Formerly of Grill 700	Harbor East
Chef Bob Whitehead	Dionysus Restaurant & Lounge	Mt. Vernon

Photo:
Annie Reid-Stone

Tapas Teatro

CHEF ANTONIO BAINES

Seared Lamb Chops

with Port Reduction & Blanched Asparagus

Serves 1-4

Lamb

9 to 11 oz.	Frenched, trimmed, silver removed lamb rack (if for 1 serving, 2 chops from large end of rack)
✓	Kosher salt, to taste
✓	freshly ground pink, green, tellicherry peppercorns, to taste
1 TB.	extra virgin olive oil
✓	fresh garlic cloves, cracked
2 springs	fresh rosemary
2 sprigs	fresh thyme

Reduction

1/2 cup	port wine
1 cup	lamb or beef stock
2 tsp.	unsalted butter
✓	pinch Kosher salt
✓	pinch peppercorn blend
1 tsp.	Dijon mustard
✓	dash Worcestershire sauce

Asparagus

✓	Fresh asparagus (white ends cut & peeled if using larger variety)

❶ Pre-heat oven to 450°.

❷ Season lamb rack with salt and pepper.

❸ In a preheated sauté pan, add olive oil, garlic cloves and rosemary and thyme sprigs. Move to side of pan after the oil is scented and then add lamb rack, flesh side down.

❹ Sear the lamb until it is evenly browned the entire length of the rack.

❺ Remove rack from pan and place on sheet pan, bone side down and place in center rack of oven for 10 to 12 minutes. Remove from oven and let rest for 10 minutes more.

❻ **To make reduction**: in same sauté pan on high heat, add the port. Once alcohol flashes off, add stock, butter, salt, pepper. Reduce to half. Add Dijon and Worcestershire and whisk until smooth. Remove herb sprigs and garlic cloves. Your reduction is ready when it covers the back of a spoon evenly.

❼ Place fresh asparagus in pot of boiling salted water for approximately 2 to 3 minutes.

❽ Remove, drain and serve immediately with lamb. Drizzle with sauce.

Try to trim your rack the day before you prepare it. Place your rosemary, thyme and cracked garlic cloves around the lamb and wrap in plastic. Refrigerate. The herbs and garlic are what you use to scent the oil and flavor your reduction.

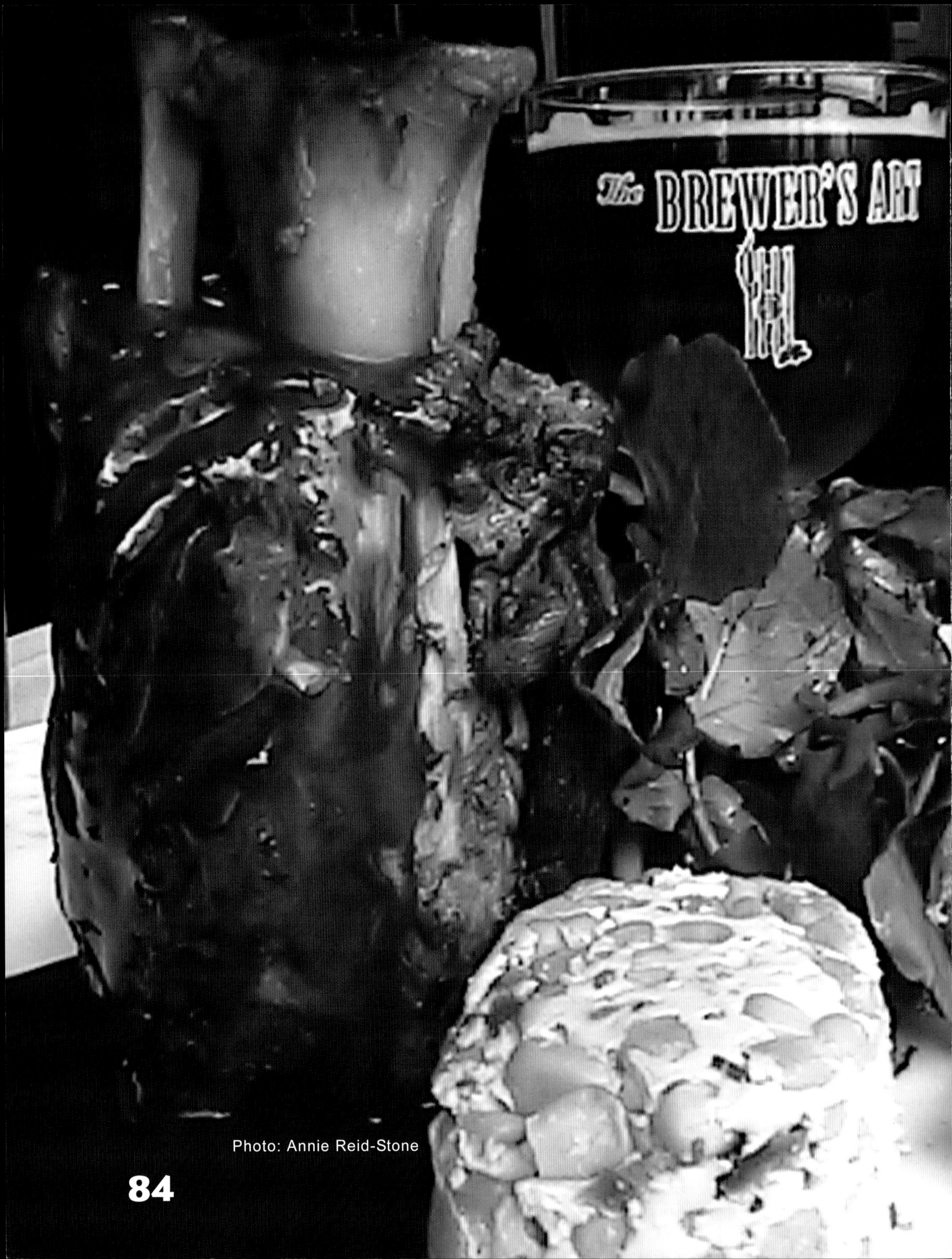

The BREWER'S ART

Photo: Annie Reid-Stone

The Brewer's Art

Chef John "Tip" Carter IV

Braised Pork Shank

with Pea Shoot & Tomato Salad, Silver Queen Corn Timbale and Natural Jus

Serves 2

2	pork shanks
2 oz.	cooking oil
2	large onions, coarse chop
2	carrots, coarse chop
2 stalks	celery, coarse chop
2	bay leaves
1 TB.	whole black pepper
2 ears	Silver Queen corn, fire roasted
2	egg yolks
1/2 cup	heavy cream
2	vine ripened tomatoes, medium dice
1/2 lb.	fresh pea shoots, medium dice
1 oz.	extra virgin olive oil
✓	salt & pepper to taste

❶Preheat oven to 375°. Place a heavy roasting pan or pot on medium flame. Add cooking oil, heat. Place pork shanks into hot pan and brown on both sides. When brown, add onions, carrots, celery, bay leaves and whole black pepper to pan. Add enough water to just cover the shanks. Loosely cover pan with foil and place in oven.

❷Cook for 3 hours or until meat is just about to fall off the bone.

❸Take shank out of braising liquid and reserve until later. Strain liquid into a sauce pan and reduce by 90% or until the liquid has consistency of a sauce. Add salt and pepper to taste.

❹**For the corn timbale:** Roast corn over open flame or grill until the kernels are golden brown. Let cool and cut kernels off the cob. Divide the corn in half and place in ceramic serving cups. Mix egg yolks and cream together with a pinch of salt and pepper and pour over the corn just until the cream mixture covers the corn. Place the cups into a shallow baking pan. Pour water into the baking pan around the cups until half way up the outside of the cups of corn (*bain marie*). Bake in 375° oven for 45 minutes or until corn has set.

❺**For the pea shoot salad:** In a mixing bowl, toss tomatoes and pea shoots together with olive oil and salt and pepper to taste.

❻**To serve:** Heat the pork shank in oven with corn timbale. Place pork shank onto plate along with half the salad. Run a knife around the edge of corn timbale and invert the cup onto the plate. Pour sauce on the shank and serve.

You may get this product at any local butcher shop or gourmet supermarket. I have my butcher "flat cut" the end of the shank so it will stand up on the plate for presentation purposes. If pea shoots are not available, any type of greens will do.

Photo courtesy of
Da Mimmo

Da Mimmo

CHEF MIMMO CRICCHIO

Broiled Veal Chop Alla Fiorentina
(Da Mimmo Signature Dish)

Serves 2

2	3" thick veal loin chops
2 cloves	garlic, chopped
1 tsp.	rosemary
1 tsp.	sage
✓	pinch salt and pepper
2 oz.	virgin olive oil
1	stick butter
1	lemon

❶ Butterfly veal chops and marinate for 2 to 3 hours in a mixture of chopped garlic, rosemary, sage, salt, pepper and olive oil.

❷ Coat veal chops thoroughly by turning several times.

❸ Put veal chops on broiling pan, coated with butter.

❹ Place pan under 350° broiler and cook veal for 5 minutes on each side.

❺ Arrange veal chops on plates and pour natural juices from pan over them. Squeeze lemon on top and serve with steamed vegetables.

This recipe is credited to my late husband, Chef Mimmo Cricchio. All of his recipes are documented and the kitchen staff that he himself trained are still executing them to perfection. I and our 14 year old son, Mimmo Jr., are continuing the tradition here at Da Mimmo. On January 11, 2005 we celebrated our 21st anniversary.

Photo courtesy of Big Steak Management

Babalu Grill
CHEF LUIS DIAZ

Ropa Vieja (Old Clothes) with *Maduros*

Shredded Braised Beef with Fried Ripe Plantains

Serves 6

2 1/4 lb.	flank steak
1 1/2 TB.	mashed garlic cloves
1 1/2 lb.	canned tomatoes, crushed
3 stalks	celery
1/4 lb.	carrots
1 1/2	onions, sliced
1 1/2	bay leaves
1 1/2 TB.	salt
1 1/2 TB.	pepper
1 1/2 TB.	cumin
1/4 bunch	fresh oregano, chopped
1/4 bunch	fresh cilantro, chopped
1/4 bunch	fresh thyme, chopped

❶ Place beef, vegetables and spices in a large pot.

❷ Cover ingredients with water.

❸ Cook over low heat for two hours, until meat is tender.

❹ Remove meat from stock (save the stock for Ropa Sauce). Allow meat to cool, then shred it.

Ropa Sauce

2 TB.	olive oil
1	onion, diced
2 TB.	minced garlic
1 qt.	canned tomatoes, crushed
2 TB.	cilantro, chopped
1 tsp.	cumin
1 tsp.	coriander
1 TB.	black pepper
1 TB.	salt
1 cup	white wine
1 cup	braised beef stock

❶ Heal oil over low heat; add onion and garlic. Cook until tender.

❷ Add tomatoes, cilantro, cumin, coriander, black pepper, salt, white wine and the reserved stock from cooking the beef.

❸ Cook for 30 minutes.

❹ Puree the sauce with a wand mixer.

Continued...

Photo courtesy of Big Steak Management

Babalu Grill
CHEF LUIS DIAZ

Ropa Vieja (continued)

Sofrito

3 TB.	olive oil
2	red peppers, seeded, cut in julienne
2	yellow peppers, seeded, cut in julienne
2	green peppers, seeded, cut in julienne
2	onions, julienne
1 TB.	minced garlic
1/4 cup	fresh cilantro, chopped
2 tsp.	cumin
2 tsp.	coriander
1 tsp.	salt
1 tsp.	pepper

❶ Heat oil over low fire.

❷ Add peppers, onions, garlic, and spices.

❸ Cook until vegetables are tender, about 6-8 minutes.

❹ Cool and refrigerate until ready to use.

Maduros

4	very ripe plantains, quartered (skin should be heavily spotted; close to black)
3 TB.	olive oil

❶ Heat oil to 375° in large skillet. Cut each plantain into 4 pieces.

❷ Fry plantains until golden brown (about 2 or 3 minutes on each side: turn with slotted spoon). Drain on paper towels and serve immediately.

To Assemble

7 oz.	Ropa Vieja
3 oz.	Sofrito
6 oz.	Ropa sauce
8 oz.	white rice, cooked
4 pieces	maduros
1 sprig	parsley
1	lime wedge
1/2	scallion, chopped

❶ Heat Ropa Vieja with sofrito and 2 ounces of sauce. Place rice in center of a decorated round plate. Place Ropa Vieja on top of rice.

❷ Place 4 slices of maduros on plate at 3, 6, 9 and 12 o'clock positions. Finish with sauce. Garnish with fresh parsley sprig, lime and chopped scallions.

Photo courtesy of Chiapparelli's Restaurant

Chiapparelli's Restaurant
CHEF RUSSEL FREW

Lamb "Bucco"

Serves 2

2	lamb shanks
✓	salt and pepper
✓	flour for coating
3 TB.	olive oil
2 cloves	garlic, peeled and chopped
1/2 cup	dry red wine
4 cups	chicken stock

❶Preheat oven to 450°.

❷Season lamb shanks with salt and pepper, then coat with flour.

❸Heat olive oil on medium high in a sauté pan and brown shanks on all sides. Remove shanks from pan and set aside.

❹Add garlic to pan and sauté until lightly browned. Deglaze pan using the red wine and scrape any bits from the bottom. Cook for 2 minutes or until alcohol has evaporated.

❺Whisk in chicken stock. Put shanks back into pan, cover and bake in oven for 2 hours; adding more chicken stock throughout the baking process when needed. Cook until meat is "falling off the bone" tender.

❻Serve with green beans and a side of gnocchi.

Photo: Annie Reid-Stone

Shula's Steak House
Chef Brian Hart

Steak Grand Marnier

Serves 4

4	4-oz. filets of beef
1 cup	olive oil, divided
1/2 tsp.	salt
1/2 tsp.	pepper
1/2 tsp.	steak seasoning
1	large onion
1 1/2 cups	Grand Marnier
1 cup	beef demi-glace
1 cup	butter

❶Preheat oven to 350°.

❷Place beef on a small pan and rub with some of the oil. Season with salt, pepper and steak seasoning.

❸Put most of remaining oil in large sauté pan over high heat. Add filets of beef. Sear on both sides.

❹Remove steaks from sauté pan and put in oven pan. Roast for 15-25 minutes in 350° oven, turning once.

❺Peel and julienne one large onion. Using same sauté pan beef was seared in, but on lower temperature, sauté onions in remaining oil until they are transparent.

❻Add Grand Marnier; cook 1 minute longer. Add beef demi; bring to a boil. Add butter to thicken.

❼Remove steaks from oven at desired doneness (shorter time for rare; longer time for well).

❽Plate, and pour pan juices over steaks.

Photo: Annie Reid-Stone

The Brass Elephant
Chef Christopher Lewis

Oven Roasted Pork with Peach Bourbon Sauce over Peach Salad

Serves 4

2 lbs.	pork, loin or chops
✓	olive oil

Dry Rub

1 TB.	salt
2 TB.	sugar
2 TB.	brown sugar
1 TB.	cumin
2 TB.	chili powder
2 TB.	mustard seed
2 TB.	Old Bay seasoning
1 TB.	Cayenne
1 TB.	cayenne pepper
1 tsp.	nutmeg
1/4 tsp.	paprika

Barbecue Sauce

1	shallot
1/4 cup	oil
1/2 cup	peach brandy
2 1/2 cups	peeled peaches (about 5)
10 1/2 oz.	can peeled tomatoes, diced
1/2 cup	corn syrup
1/2 cup	cider vinegar
1/2 cup	brown sugar
1 TB.	dry mustard
1 TB.	Worcestershire sauce
1 1/2 tsp.	paprika
1/2 tsp.	salt
1/2 tsp.	garlic powder
1/2 tsp.	black pepper

❶Mix ingredients for dry rub together; rub on meat and let marinate overnight in refrigerator.

❷Heat oil in pan; add meat and sear on all sides until crust forms. Finish in 325° oven for 15 minutes.

❸**Barbecue Sauce:** Sauté shallot in oil for one minute. Add peach brandy (it will ignite). When flame subsides, add remaining ingredients.

❹Simmer for 20 minutes. Puree, discarding bulk.

❺**Salad:** Brown peaches in oven on oiled pan. Toss with rest of salad ingredients.

❻To plate, place salad at center of platter. Slice loin and arrange around salad. Drizzle barbecue sauce over the meat.

Peach Salad

✓	Microgreens
✓	Sliced, peeled peaches
1	Red onion, diced
✓	Fresh cilantro
✓	Brown sugar
✓	Cayenne pepper

Photo: Annie Reid-Stone

Sabatino's Italian Restaurant

CHEF RENATO ROTONDO, SR.

Veal Francese a la Sabatino

Serves 4

2	eggs, beaten
✓	pinch of fresh parsley
✓	pinch of salt
✓	pinch of pepper
1/2 cup	Half and Half
1 1/2 cups	bread crumbs
1 1/2 lbs.	veal scallopine, sliced
3 TB.	butter
4 TB.	oil
2 TB.	flour
3/4 cup	Sherry
✓	juice of 1/4 lemon
3/4 cup	chicken broth
4 slices	lemon

❶ Combine eggs, parsley, salt, pepper and Half and Half to make batter.

❷ Place bread crumbs in a separate bowl.

❸ Place each slice of veal between layers of waxed paper and pound thin. Dip veal into egg batter, and then coat both sides with bread crumbs, shaking off loose breading.

❹ In a heavy skillet, heat butter with oil, and fry coated veal until it is golden brown. Remove veal and set aside on warm platter.

❺ Add flour to pan and stir until brown. Add Sherry and lemon juice, then chicken broth. Simmer for 3 minutes.

❻ Pour over fried veal and garnish with lemon slices.

Photo courtesy of Grill 700

Tenderloin Filet
& Charred Tomato Salad with Rosti Potato

Serves 4

4	filet mignon, 8 ounces each
1	Idaho or Russet potato, washed
4 oz.	olive oil, divided
✓	Kosher salt (optional)
✓	fresh cracked black pepper (optional)
6	tomatoes (vine-ripened)
1	red onion
4 TB.	garlic, minced
1 TB.	Chiptole pepper, minced
3 oz.	red wine vinegar
3 TB.	basil, chiffonade (cut into fine strips, or minced)
2 TB.	thyme and chives, chopped
1 oz.	leeks, julienne, fried
1 oz.	basil oil

❶ **Rosti Potato:** Preheat oven to 350°. Preheat a heavy gauge sauté pan over moderate heat. While pan is heating, slice potato 1/8" thick. Add 1 ounce olive oil to pan and shingle each potato slice off one another, in a circle. Season with salt and pepper and cook until bottom is golden brown.

❷ With spatula, carefully flip the potato rosti over and brown. Once golden, finish potatoes in oven until cooked through (~15 minutes).

❸ Once cooked, remove potato rosti from pan and cut into four triangles.

❹ **Charred Tomato Salad:** Thickly slice tomatoes and red onions (1" thick), brush with olive oil and grill on both sides until lightly charred. Remove and chop into bite-size pieces.

❺ In a pot over medium heat, sauté 3 tablespoons garlic in olive oil for one minute. Add chiptole and red wine vinegar and reduce by half. Once reduced, add chopped onion and tomatoes. Simmer 10 minutes. Season with salt & pepper, top with fresh basil chiffonade.

❻ **Filet:** Mix together 1 tablespoon garlic, 1 ounce olive oil and 2 tablespoons thyme and chives. Rub filet mignon in this mixture, to cover completely. Drain excess oil and grill the fillet on both sides for a few minutes. Finish cooking in a 350° degree oven until desired doneness.

❼ **For Plating:** Place charred tomato salad in center of plate. Top with filet. Lean Potato Rosti against filet, then finish with fried leeks over filet. Basil oil is an optional garnish.

Dionysus Restaurant & Lounge

Chef Bob Whitehead

Pork Tenderloin Scallops
with Apricot & Green Peppercorn Sauce

Serves 4

16 oz.	pork tenderloin
3 TB.	butter
✓	flour for dredging
1 TB.	shallots (or red onion) diced fine
2 cloves	garlic, diced fine
2 TB.	green peppercorns
6 oz.	dried apricots, rough chopped
2 oz.	white wine
6 oz.	chicken broth (stock)
✓	salt and pepper to taste

❶Clean the tenderloin, removing all visible fat and silverskin. Cut the loin across the grain into ½ inch thick slices (16 pieces).

❷Place the pork between 2 pieces of plastic wrap and pound lightly with a meat tenderizer or heavy sauce pan (be careful not to tear or pound holes in the meat).

❸Heat a sauté pan (frying pan) and add the butter. Wait for bubbles to stop.

❹Dredge the pork in flour and place in sauté pan. Sauté for 1 minute then flip over and add shallots, garlic, peppercorns and apricots. Cook one minute more, stirring.

❺Add wine, reduce for a few seconds. Add chicken stock and allow to reduce for 1 to 2 minutes. Add salt and pepper to taste.

❻Place 4 pieces of pork on each plate, one overlapping the other. Spoon some of the sauce with apricots and peppercorns on top. Serve with your favorite rice or potatoes, and fresh vegetables.

I picked this recipe because the ingredients can be found in any grocery store and it can easily be prepared in about 15 minutes. This dish is also great in any season.

Photo: Annie Reid-Stone

Poultry

Poultry is always found on menus in Baltimore, even in seafood and steak houses: that's because it is sure to please everyone. The selection here includes chicken, duck, quail and turkey, all by some of the great chefs of Baltimore.

Chef	Restaurant	Location
John "Tip" Carter IV	The Brewer's Art	Mt. Vernon
Rey Eugenio	Roy's Restaurant of Baltimore	Harbor East
Rashed Edwards	Mezze	Fell's Point
Steve Francis	The Chameleon Café	Lauraville
Nino Germano	La Scala Ristorante	Little Italy
Eric Huckleberry	Ryan's Daughter	Belevedere Square
CBrian Martin	Mezze	Fell's Point
Franklin Thomas	George's, Peabody Court Hotel	Mt. Vernon
Frances Thompson	George's, Peabody Court Hotel	Mt. Vernon
Eric Yeager	Baldwin's Station	Sykesville

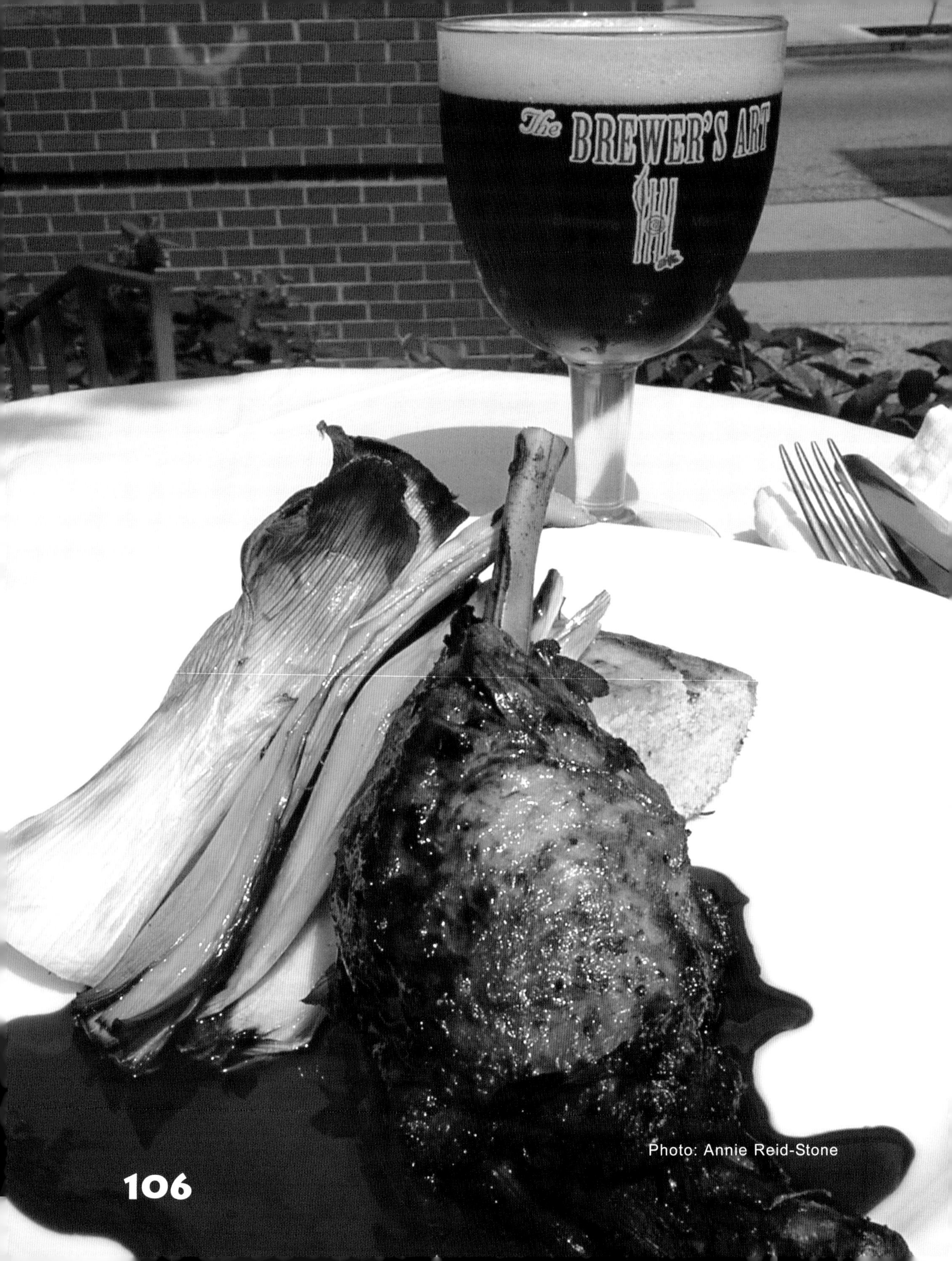

Photo: Annie Reid-Stone

The Brewer's Art

CHEF JOHN "TIP" CARTER IV

Sour Cherry Braised Duck Leg

with Cherry Sauce, Pan Fried Cornbread & Roasted Leeks

Serves 4

4	Hudson Valley duck legs
2 cups	diced onions
1 cup	diced carrots
1 cup	diced celery
1 bunch	fresh thyme
1 oz.	whole black peppers
4	bay leaves
2 qts.	chicken stock
1 lb.	sour cherry puree (or hydrated dried cherry puree)
✓	salt and pepper
12	leeks

Braised Duck Sauce (1 quart)

2 qts.	cherry braising liquid
1 bunch	thyme
4	bay leaves
3 TB.	flour
3 TB.	butter, softened
✓	salt and pepper

Pan Fried Cornbread

2 cups	white corn meal (self-rising)
1/2 cup	buttermilk
✓	salt & pepper
2 TB.	cooking oil

❶Preheat oven to 350°. In heavy braising pan, sear duck legs until golden brown on both sides. Add the rest of the ingredients, with the exception of salt and pepper. Cover pan with lid or foil. Place in oven for 2 1/2 hours, checking often. Add more chicken stock or water as needed to keep the duck legs submerged.

❷After braising, remove duck legs from liquid and place on a cooling rack. Refrigerate. Strain braising liquid and reserve for the sauce.

❸**Sauce:** Place braising liquid in a heavy sauce pot with thyme and bay leaves. Reduce liquid by half and thicken with mixture of flour and butter that have been kneaded together. Add salt and pepper to taste.

❹**Cornbead:** Heat a cast iron skillet to 425° in oven. Mix together corn meal, buttermilk, salt and pepper. Add cooking oil to the hot skillet. Pour cornbread mixture into skillet; place in hot oven and bake for 45 to 50 minutes, or until bread is brown on top.

❺**Leeks:** Preheat oven to 350°. Split leeks lengthwise, place on sheet pan with a little olive oil, and roast until they are slightly browned.

❻**To Plate:** Place slice of cornbread on plate. Lean 6 leek halves against the cornbread. Lean duck leg against leeks and bread. Pour sauce down the duck leg.

Photo: Annie Reid-Stone

Roy's Restaurant of Baltimore
CHEF REY EUGENIO

Jade Pesto Baked Stuffed Quail

with Coconut-Ginger Sweet Potatoes and Thai Peanut-Chili Sauce

Serves 4

Sweet Potato Mash

2	sweet potatoes
✓	Coconut milk to cover sweet potatoes
2 TB.	butter at room temperature
1 TB.	minced ginger
✓	salt and pepper to taste

Thai Peanut-Chili Sauce

1 cup	coconut milk (use reserved from sweet potatoes)
2 TB.	brown sugar
1 TB.	soy sauce
2 tsp.	fish sauce
1/4 cup	sweet onions
1 tsp.	dried chili flakes (more, for added heat)
1/4 cup	chopped cilantro
1/4 cup	chopped Thai basil
3	minced kaffir lime leaves
1 TB.	minced lemongrass
2 tsp.	minced garlic
2 tsp.	minced ginger
1 TB.	freshly squeezed lime juice
1 TB.	rice wine vinegar
1/2 cup	creamy peanut butter

❶Peel and dice sweet potatoes and place in a saucepot.

❷Add just enough coconut milk to cover potatoes. Bring to a simmer.

❸When potatoes are fork tender strain them, reserving coconut milk.

❹Place cooked potatoes, soft butter and minced ginger in a mixing bowl and mash with a fork or potato masher. Add some of the coconut milk to make it creamy. Season with salt and pepper.

❺Cover and keep warm. Reserve remaining coconut milk for Thai Peanut Chili Sauce.

❻**Sauce:** Place all ingredients into a saucepot and blend well with a whisk over medium-high heat; bring to a slow boil.

❼Reduce heat to medium-low and simmer for 25-30 minutes.

❽Strain sauce through a fine mesh sieve and keep warm.

Continued...

Photo: Annie Reid-Stone

Roy's Restaurant of Baltimore
CHEF REY EUGENIO

Baked Stuffed Quail (continued)

Stuffed Quail

4	quails
✓	vegetable oil
1/2 cup	sweet onions, julienne
1/4 cup	fennel, julienne
1/4 cup	shitake mushrooms, julienne
3 oz.	Boursin cheese

Jade Pesto

1 bunch	cilantro (roughly chopped)
1/4 cup	oyster sauce
1 TB.	sesame oil
1 tsp.	fish sauce
2 tsp.	chopped garlic
2 tsp.	chopped ginger

❶ To prepare quails, cut off leg portions and place into small saucepan. Add just enough vegetable oil to cover.

❷ Place over medium-low heat for 15-20 minutes.

❸ Remove from heat, let cool. When cool enough to handle, pick leg meat and set aside.

❹ Lightly caramelize the onions, fennel and mushrooms, then chill.

❺ Add leg meat and Boursin cheese, season with salt and pepper and mix well.

❻ Preheat oven to 325° F.

❼ **Jade Pesto:** Place all ingredients into a blender. Blend well into a light paste.

❽ Divide meat mixture into 4 portions and stuff each quail breast with it.

❾ Brush the Jade Pesto onto each quail breast and oven bake for 10 to 12 minutes.

❿ To serve, divide the sweet onions onto 4 plates. Gently slice each quail breast down the center to expose stuffing and place on top of sweet potato mash. Spoon each dish with Thai Peanut-Chili Sauce and a small amount onto each quail breast. Serve with your choice of fresh vegetables and garnish with fried wonton chips.

Jade pesto can be used on any poultry product of your choice, even on fresh fish or shellfish. To simplify this recipe, chicken breast alone would be great, served on a bed of mixed greens as a salad course or a light entrée.

Photo: Annie Reid-Stone

The Chameleon Café
CHEF STEVE FRANCIS

Chicken Maryland

Serves 4

1	whole chicken
2 cups	bread crumbs
1/2 cup	flour
1	egg
2 tsp.	salt
1/4 tsp.	black pepper
1/2 TB.	celery seed
2 TB.	water
✓	oil for frying
5 slices	bacon
2	bananas

Horseradish Sauce

1 TB.	butter
2 TB.	flour
1 cup	chicken stock
1/2 cup	heavy cream
1 tsp.	vinegar
1 tsp.	dry mustard
2 TB.	prepared horseradish
✓	salt and pepper to taste

❶**Horseradish Sauce:** Melt butter in a saucepan. When melted, add flour. Cook until lightly browned. Add stock and stir. Simmer for 5 minutes. Add cream. Mix mustard and vinegar together; add to sauce. Finish with horseradish, salt and pepper. Simmer while chicken cooks.

❷**Chicken:** Quarter chicken. Place breadcrumbs, flour, and egg in separate bowls. Mix salt and pepper with the breadcrumbs. Add water and celery seed to egg and beat. Dip each piece of chicken in the flour, then in the egg, then in the breadcrumbs. Pan fry chicken in oil until browned and cooked through.

❸**Garnish:** Render bacon until crisp. Pull out of pan and reserve. Pour off all but 2 tablespoons of the fat. Peel and split bananas. Fry bananas in the 2 tablespoons of bacon fat until soft and brown. Serve with chicken and sauce.

This is a revised version of the classic French dish "Poulet Saute Maryland" from the cookbook Escoffier, The Complete Guide to the Art of Modern Cookery. We believe the use of bananas in a dish with Maryland in its name pays homage to Maryland's past.

Photo: Annie Reid-Stone

La Scala Ristorante
CHEF NINO GERMANO

Pollo alla Scala

Sauteed Chicken, Artichoke Hearts and Lump Crab Meat in White Wine Sauce

Serves 2

2 6-oz.	skinless and boneless chicken breasts, flattened
✓	flour, for dusting
1 1/2 oz.	olive oil
2	artichoke hearts (canned), split into quarters
2 oz.	jumbo lump crab meat
3 oz.	white wine
✓	juice of half a lemon
✓	salt and pepper to taste
1/2 oz.	butter

❶ Dust each chicken breast in flour.

❷ In sauté pan, heat olive oil; place chicken breasts in pan and sauté until brown on both sides.

❸ Reduce heat and add artichoke hearts, crab meat, white wine, lemon juice and salt and pepper to taste.

❹ Cook until liquid reduces and chicken is done.

❺ Finish by adding butter to pan and turning chicken to coat.

All ingredients are imported from Italy and can be found in Little Italy at Il Scalino, at 313 South High Street. (www.ilscalino.com)

Photo: Annie Reid-Stone

Ryan's Daughter
Chef Eric Huckleberry

Cottage Pie

Serves 5

Champ (Irish Mashed Potatoes)

1 lb.	Idaho potatoes, peeled and quartered
1/2 pint	sour cream
8	spring onions, trimmed keeping onion and half of green tops
4 oz.	Kerrygold butter
✓	salt and white pepper
6 TB.	butter
6 TB.	flour

Pie

2 oz.	olive oil
1	yellow onion, small dice
4	carrots, small dice
1 bunch	celery, small dice
3 TB.	minced garlic
3 qts.	chicken stock
1 qt.	heavy cream
1 bag	mixed vegetables
2 lbs.	chicken, white meat only, cooked and shredded
✓	salt and white pepper
1 lb.	Kerrygold Smoked Blarney Castle Cheese, shredded

❶**Champ:** Boil potatoes in lightly salted water until tender. Strain through a colander until dry. Place potatoes in a mixer and add sour cream, green onions and butter. Mix well. Season with salt and white pepper. (Careful, white pepper is strong).

❷**Roux:** Melt the butter in a pot on low heat; add equal part flour and mix for 7 minutes over medium-low heat. Put to the side and reserve.

❸**Pie:** Sauté onions, carrots, celery and garlic in the olive oil in a stock pot. Cook for 10 minutes, until the onions are translucent and the smell of the garlic is aromatic. Add the chicken stock and bring to a boil on high heat. Add the heavy cream and lower the flame to medium-high and reduce by one-third. Whisk in the roux and start to thicken. While thickening, add mixed veggies. Turn off the heat when thickened and add cooked chicken. Season with salt and pepper.

❹Preheat oven to 375°.

❺Place stew in a casserole dish. Put the cooled mashed potatoes into a pastry bag and pipe onto the stew. If a pastry bag isn't available, pat the potatoes with your hands into a disc form to cover the casserole dish and then top with the shredded Blarney Castle cheese. Bake until the cheese has melted and the potatoes are hot. Serve!

This dish is a favorite at Ryan's Daughter. I like it because it's different than Chicken Pot Pie and the creamy texture of the stew with the Champ and Irish cheese really brings out a wonderful flavor for the palette.

Photo: Scott T. Mislan

Mezze

CHEFS BRIAN MARTIN / RASHED EDWARDS

Kleftico

Serves 6

6	chicken thighs with skin
3 cloves	garlic, minced
1/8 cup	olive oil
1/4 tsp.	salt
1/8 tsp.	black pepper
1 TB.	sugar
✓	juice of 1 lemon
1/2 cup	white wine
1 small	diced carrot
1 cup	peas
1/8 tsp.	dried oregano
1	small white onion, diced
1	tomato (diced)
1	potato, fried (diced)
1/2 cup	grated Parmesan cheese
3/4 cup	grated Kaseri cheese
1/2 cup	yogurt
6	sheets phyllo #10
1/2 cup	butter, melted

❶Place chicken, one garlic clove, half of the oil, salt, pepper, sugar, lemon juice and wine in a pot. Simmer 40 to 50 minutes, covered.

❷In a separate pot, add remaining oil and sweat carrot for five minutes. Then add 1 clove garlic, peas, oregano, onion, tomato, fried potato cubes and simmer 5 more minutes.

❸Pull chicken from pot and strain liquid into vegetable pot. Simmer the vegetables in chicken liquid for 15 minutes.

❹Pull meat from chicken (remove skin). Fry the chicken skin until crisp, then chop into small pieces.

❺Cool vegetable mixture slightly, then add cheeses, chicken skin, chicken and yogurt. Season to taste.

❻**To Finish:** Preheat oven to 350°. Spread phyllo sheets separately on table, brush with melted butter. Fold right side of sheet over to left side. Brush with butter again. Divide chicken mixture onto the six sheets, slightly higher in center. Bring top of phyllo down over chicken mixture, then fold sides over the mix and roll chicken mix towards your body until fully wrapped.

❼Place wraps on cookie sheet. Brush top of kleftico with butter and make two small incisions with a toothpick.

❽Bake in oven for approximately 20 minutes.

Photo: Annie Reid-Stone

George's, Peabody Court Hotel
CHEF FRANKLIN THOMAS

Fried Buttermilk Organic Chicken

with Braised Napa Cabbage & Buttermilk Béchamel Sauce

Serves 4

Béchamel Sauce

8 oz.	unsalted butter
1/2 cup	all purpose flour
1/2 qt.	buttermilk
✓	salt and white pepper

Cabbage

✓	Oil for sautéing
1 tsp.	minced shallots
1/2 cup	white wine
2 TB.	honey
2 cups	chicken stock
2 lbs.	Napa cabbage, sliced
✓	Kosher salt & pepper

Chicken

4	chicken breast halves (bone in and skin on)
1 1/4 cups	buttermilk
1/2 cup	flour
1 tsp.	salt & pepper
1/4 cup	vegetable oil
✓	micro greens
1/4 lb.	basil, julienne

❶ **Sauce:** Melt butter over low heat in medium saucepan. Once foaming, add all the flour, mixing well with wooden spoon. Cook over low heat 3-4 mins, stirring constantly to incorporate and cook flour, forming a roux.

❷ Remove pan from heat and let stand for 15 minutes. Meanwhile, in medium saucepan, scald buttermilk (heating it until just below boiling point). Return pan with roux to medium-low heat. Add all of the scalded buttermilk at once (to avoid the formation of lumps). Simmer, stirring gently with a wooden spoon. Cook, stirring, over low heat, 15 to 20 minutes, until smooth and thickened. Strain sauce through fine-mesh strainer. Season with salt and white pepper.

❷ **Cabbage:** Preheat oven to 400°. Place medium-size roasting pan on burner over medium-high heat; add oil and sweat shallots. Add white wine and reduce. Place cabbage in roasting pan with shallots, stir in honey and chicken stock and season with salt and pepper. Cover with foil and roast in oven until wilted, about 30 mins. Remove from the oven. Transfer to a platter.

❸ Place chicken breast halves in a bowl; pour buttermilk over top and marinate at least 1 hour. In another bowl, mix flour, salt and pepper. Remove chicken from buttermilk and roll into flour mix. Pour oil into skillet. Cook chicken in hot oil until one side is browned; then turn and brown the other side (about 20 minutes total). Remove chicken and place on paper towels to drain.

❹ Plate up! Ladle sauce in the center of each of 4 plates; place a mound of cabbage in the center of the sauce (made sure it's drained), then stack equal pieces of chicken atop the cabbage. Garnish with micro greens and basil.

Photo: Annie Reid-Stone

George's, Peabody Court Hotel
CHEF FRANCES THOMPSON

George Washington Sandwich

Serves 1

4 oz.	turkey breast, sliced
1 oz.	Sage cheddar cheese
1 oz.	Focaccia bread
✓	Cranberry Mayonnaise (below)
✓	lettuce, tomatoes (optional)

Cranberry Mayonnaise

2 oz.	mayonnaise
1 oz.	dry cranberries
1 tsp.	cranberry juice

❶**Cranberry Mayonnaise:** Combine all the ingredients and mix well.

❷Spread Focaccia bread with the cranberry mayonnaise.

❸Build sandwich of turkey and cheddar cheese.

❹Add lettuce and tomatoes as desired.

❺Serve with your favorite side dish and enjoy!

Photo:
Annie Reid-Stone

Baldwin's Station
CHEF ERIC YEAGER

Herb Roasted Duck with Strawberry and Arugula Salad

Serves 4

2	8-oz. duck breasts
1 tsp.	thyme
✓	salt and pepper to taste
2	cloves garlic, finely minced
2 tsp.	chopped rosemary, divided
4 oz.	balsamic vinegar , divided
4 oz.	vegetable oil, divided
4 oz.	dried cranberries
1 oz.	honey
✓	salt and pepper to taste
8 oz.	arugula
4 oz.	goat cheese
4 oz.	diced walnuts
1/2 pint	strawberries

❶Place duck on a clean dry surface. In a small mixing bowl, add the thyme, salt, pepper, and one finely minced garlic clove. Add 1 tsp of rosemary once well incorporated. Sprinkle the rub onto the duck and let sit in the fridge while you start the dressing.

❷**Dressing:** In a blender, combine 2 oz. balsamic vinegar, 2 oz. vegetable oil, the remaining rosemary, 2 oz. cranberries, and honey. You don't want to blend it entirely. Then, place dressing in a container and add in the remaining cranberries, balsamic vinegar and oil. Add salt and pepper to taste. This will give the dressing different layers of flavor and body, as well.

❸Place a pan on medium high heat with vegetable oil. Take the duck out of the fridge. When the pan is hot, place the two breasts in the pan and sauté for about 3 minutes on each side - you don't want to cook it well done. While duck is cooking, start the salad.

❹**Salad:** In a large salad bowl, place the arugula, half of the goat cheese, half of the walnuts, and half of the strawberries. Add in the dressing as desired, lightly toss and plate. Drizzle the rest of the dressing that's left in the bowl on top. Use the remaining walnuts, goat cheese and strawberries to garnish. When the duck is done, slice and place on top of salad.

In Roman times, arugula was considered an aphrodisiac. They may have been right - you'll fall in love with this innovative way to serve duck. Perhaps this is why the Washington Post said Baldwin's Station was "worth the trip."

Seafood

Great seafood includes not only those fish caught fresh and grilled over an open fire, but fresh fish that is enhanced by creative cooking. In Baltimore, known for its Chesapeake Bay crab cakes, there are restaurants and chefs known for doing great things with fish and shellfish. In this section, you'll find a wonderful array of delicious traditional and creative seafood recipes.

Chef	Restaurant	Location
Richard Cook	Ruth's Chris Steakhouse-Pier 5	Inner Harbor
Mimmo Cricchio	Da Mimmo	Little Italy
Christina D'Angelo	Zodiac Restaurant	Station North
Christian deLutis	Corks	Federal Hill
Rashed Edwards	Kali's Court	Fell's Point
Rey Eugenio	Roy's Restaurant of Baltimore	Harbor East
Nate Finney	Hampton's	Inner Harbor
Russell Frew	Chiapparelli's Restaurant	Little Italy
Brian Greene	Restaurant "b"	Bolton Hill
Edwin "Zeus" Herman	Brighton's Orangerie	Inner Harbor
Troy Jones	Shula's Steak House	Downtown
Dennis Marcoux	Phillips Harborplace Restaurant	Inner Harbor
Brian Martin	Kali's Court	Fell's Point
Tim Mullen	Grill 700	Harbor East
Ravi Narayanan	Formerly of The Brewer's Art	Mt. Vernon
Felix Nuñez	Window's Restaurant	Inner Harbor
Chris Patternote	Vin Restaurant	Towson
Renato Rotondo, Sr.	Sabatino's Italian Restaurant	Little Italy
Emilio Sanz	Tío Pepe Restaurant	Mt. Vernon
Tom Schwarzweller	Crossroads Restaurant	Cross Keys
John Shields	Gertrude's	Wyman Park
Ted Stelzenmuller	Red Fish	Canton
Bryan Sullivan	Formerly of Bistro 888	Fells Point
Sonny Sweetman	Abacrombie Fine Foods	Cultural District
Graham Weber	Formerly of Grill 700	Harbor East
Cindy Wolf	Charleston	Fell's Point
Eric Yeager	Baldwin's Station	Sykesville
Joshua Young	Intercontinental Harbor Court Hotel	Inner Harbor

Photo courtesy of Big Steak Management

Ruth's Chris Steakhouse-Pier 5

CHEF RICHARD COOK

Sizzling Ahi Tuna & Colossal Crabmeat Stack

Serves 2

1 oz.	canola oil
2 TB.	blackening seasoning
2	Ahi tuna filets (5-oz each)
1/2 TB.	melted butter
2 oz.	Colossal or jumbo lump crabmeat
1 tsp.	chopped garlic
1 TB.	lemon butter (recipe follows)
1 TB.	roasted pepper pesto (recipe follows)
1 TB.	fresh red Bell pepper, 1/8" dice
✓	chopped fresh parsley
1	lemon

Roasted Red Pepper Base

1 lb.	whole red Bell peppers
1/4 oz	Canola oil
1 TB.	roasted garlic, pureed
1 TB.	salt
2 tsp.	black pepper

❶Place oil in one pie tin and blackening seasoning in another pie tin. Dip the two filets into the oil on both sides, then into the seasoning on both sides. Place into a clean, hot cast iron skillet. Cook to a medium rare temperature while blackening on both sides.

❷While tuna is cooking, remove a hot pie tin from the oven and add melted butter to the pan. Add crabmeat and garlic and place under broiler to heat. Cook for about two minutes.

❸Pre-heat oven to 400°.

❹Preparing Roasted Red Pepper Base: Wash and dry peppers well. Place on sheet pan and drizzle with oil. Toss well to coat peppers. Place in oven for 10 minutes or until peppers are roasted and skin peels off easily. Remove peppers from oven and place into refrigerator to cool. (This can be done day before, but pepper must cool for two hours). Remove skin and seeds from peppers. Place peeled peppers into a food processor and puree into a paste. You will have to do this in batches.

❺Stop food processor and scrape down sides of the bowl. Add roasted garlic puree, salt and pepper and mix until all ingredients are fully incorporated. Remove from bowl and place into a container. Add other batches of puree pepper and mix well. Refrigerate until ready to use.

Continued...

Photo courtesy of Big Steak Management

Ruth's Chris Steakhouse-Pier 5
CHEF RICHARD COOK

Sizzling Ahi Tuna (continued)

Roasted Red Pepper Pesto

1/2 cup	roasted pepper base
1/4 oz.	(2 large) garlic cloves
1/2 oz.	red onion, small dice
2 oz.	olive oil
1/2 oz.	Romano cheese
1/4 tsp.	salt
1/4 tsp.	black pepper

Lemon Butter

2 TB.	fresh lemon juice
1	stick unsalted butter, soft

❻**Preparing Red Pepper Pesto:** In a food processor, put roasted red pepper base, garlic, and onions. Process into a paste. While machine is running slowly, add olive oil. Stop processor and scrape down sides of the bowl. Add cheese, salt and pepper and process until all ingredients are fully incorporated. Remove from bowl; place in container and refrigerate until needed.

❼**Preparing Lemon Butter:** Mix butter and lemon juice together in a small bowl. Place in a squirt bottle and hold at room temperature until needed. (Any leftover lemon butter can be chilled and used within two days).

❽**To plate:** On a warm oval platter, place one of the blackened tuna filets in center. Using tongs, place half the hot crabmeat onto the filet. Place the other tuna filet on a cutting board. Cut in half on a 45-degree angle. Then crisscross the two cut pieces of tuna on top of the other tuna filet and crabmeat. The medium rare of the cut tuna should be showing. Sprinkle the remaining crabmeat around the base of the tuna and pour the butter in the pan over the tuna and crabmeat.

❾Drizzle the lemon butter over the crabmeat and tuna filets. Then drizzle 1 tablespoon of the roasted pepper pesto over the tuna and platter. Sprinkle diced peppers over the tuna and the platter; then sprinkle parsley over all.

❿Serve immediately, squeezing lemon over fish tableside.

NOTE: Make sure you have a good base of crabmeat on the bottom tuna, so you will have a good stack.

Photo courtesy of Da Mimmo

Da Mimmo

CHEF MIMMO CRICCHIO

Fungi Portabella Farci con Carne de Granchi

(Portabella Mushroom Broiled with Crabmeat Topping)

Serves 4

1 lb.	jumbo lump crabmeat, picked through for shells
1	egg, beaten
1 TB.	mayonnaise
1 tsp.	dry mustard
6	unsalted crackers, crushed
1 tsp.	Old Bay seasoning
2-4	dashes Worcestershire sauce
4	Portabella mushrooms (large - 4"in diameter), stems removed
1 tsp.	butter
✓	paprika, to taste
✓	sliced lemon, tomato, or cucumber (to garnish)

❶ Place the crab into a medium bowl.

❷ In a separate bowl, combine egg, mayonnaise, mustard, crackers, Old Bay seasoning, and Worcestershire sauce. Mix well. Gently fold mixture into the crab.

❸ Place crab mixture equally on top of each Portabella mushroom. Top each center of the stuffing with 1/4 tsp. of butter.

❹ Refrigerate for 2 hours.

❺ Preheat oven to 380°.

❻ Bake for 15 minutes. Then place under a broiler for 2 minutes. Sprinkle with paprika. Serve with your favorite garnish, perhaps sliced lemon, tomato or cucumber.

❼ The crab mixture can be made as a crab cake, without the mushroom, and fried or broiled.

This recipe is credited to my late husband, Chef Mimmo Cricchio. All of his recipes are documented and the kitchen staff that he, himself, trained are still executing them to perfection. I and our 13 year old son Mimmo Jr. are continuing the tradition here at Da Mimmo. On January 11, 2005, we celebrated our 21st anniversary.

Photo: Annie Reid-Stone

Chef Christina D'Angelo
ZODIAC RESTAURANT

Grilled Chesapeake Bay Rockfish
with Fresh Herbs, Old Bay & Crawfish Cream

Serves 4

4 8-oz.	Rockfish filets
1 cup	flour
✓	clarified butter or olive oil
2 tsp.	chopped garlic
2 tsp.	chopped shallots
1/2 lb.	crawfish tail meat
1/2 cup	dry sherry
2 tsp.	Old Bay seasoning
1 TB.	chopped dill
1 TB.	chopped thyme
1 TB.	chopped basil
1 TB.	chopped Italian parsley
1/2 cup	heavy cream
✓	salt and pepper to taste

❶ Preheat oven to 350°.

❷ Salt and pepper both sides of Rockfish filets. Dredge in flour. Sauté in butter or oil over medium heat until golden brown.

❸ Place filets on baking sheet in 350° oven. Prepare sauce while they bake.

❹ Drain all but 2 tablespoons oil from sauté pan. Over medium heat, add garlic, shallots and crawfish. Sauté for 2 minutes.

❺ Add sherry, Old Bay, and herbs. Let simmer for 1 minute longer. Add heavy cream and continue cooking until thickened. Season to taste with salt and pepper.

❻ Pour sauce over Rockfish and serve.

I love using crawfish in this recipe but for a true Maryland flavor, try substituting crab, shrimp or oysters for the crawfish.

Photo: Annie Reid-Stone

Corks

CHEF CHRISTIAN DELUTIS

House-Smoked Local Trout Two Ways

Smoked Trout Salad and Trout & Smoked Almond Mousse

3 lbs.	fresh trout

Brine

1gal.	spring water
1 cup	brown sugar
3 oz.	molasses
1 cup	Kosher salt
2	cinnamon sticks
4	allspice berries
1tsp.	pink peppercorns
3	cloves
1	bay leaf
1tsp.	fennel seed

Smoke

1 cup	sugar
1 TB.	dried lavender
5	bay leafs, crushed
1 tsp.	fennel seed

Smoked trout salad

1 1/2 lbs.	smoked trout, flaked from skin
1/2 cup	fresh aioli, or prepared mayonnaise
1 tsp.	capers
1/4 cup	red onion, diced
1 tsp.	fresh dill, chopped
1 tsp.	fresh chives, chopped
3 oz.	golden trout roe

Smoked Trout Mousse

6 oz.	cream cheese
1	lemon zest & juice
3 oz.	smoked almonds
1 1/2 lbs.	smoked trout flaked from skin
1 sheet	toasted Nori, cut into triangles

Serves 4

❶**Brine:** combine all ingredients and bring to a simmer. Cool to room temperature, then add trout (head and tail removed) and refrigerate for 2 days. Once brined for 2 days, remove trout and rinse gently.

❷**To Smoke:** Fill 1 pan* with dry spices and sugar, place a greased wire resting rack over spices and cover with second pan. Place pan on high heat. Once smoke appears, place trout on rack, cover, and smoke 10 minutes. Allow trout to cool once removed from smoke, then flake from skin for further preparation.

❸**Trout salad:** Take half of flaked trout, gently toss with aioli, then fold in other ingredients. Salt & pepper to taste.

❹**Smoked Trout Mousse:** Pulse cream cheese, lemon juice, zest, and almonds in a food processor till smooth. Next add trout and puree till desired consistency.

❺**To plate:** we generally mold our trout salad in a cylinder shape and top with roe and greens; for the mousse we either make quenelle shape or simply pipe it through a pastry bag and garnish with toasted nori, almonds, capers, and aioli.

* *Obtain two half-hotel (sheet) pans lined with foil, or two 12" x 9" disposable aluminum pans*

Photo:
Annie Reid-Stone

Roy's Restaurant of Baltimore

CHEF REY EUGENIO

Franchaise of Halibut

with Melted Roma Tomato Petals & Curried Tomato Broth

Serves 4

Melted Roma Tomatoes

10	Roma tomatoes
1/4 cup	red onion, fine julienne
1/4 cup	fennel, fine julienne
1	yellow Bell pepper, fine julienne
1/2 cup	mung bean sprouts
1/4 cup	picked Thai basil leaves

Curried Tomato Broth

✓	tomato & vegetable trimmings
1/2 cup	chopped celery
1 stalk	lemongrass, chopped
1 TB.	tomato paste
✓	Thai basil and cilantro stems
1 tsp.	red curry paste (or more)
4	garlic cloves, crushed
1	small ginger root, sliced
✓	Filtered water to cover
✓	Salt and pepper

Franchaise Batter

2	whole eggs
1/4 cup	heavy cream
2 TBS.	grated Parmesan cheese
1 TB.	chopped chives
1 TB.	chopped cilantro

Fish Filets

4	fish filets (5 to 7 ounces each)
✓	all purpose flour seasoned with salt and white pepper
✓	clarified butter or vegetable oil

Garnish

✓	Chive sticks and Nori strips

❶ Quarter each tomato. Remove pulp and carefully skin each tomato petal. Reserve all vegetable trimmings for later. Place all ingredients in medium saucepot and set aside.

❷ **Tomato Broth:** Place all ingredients in a large saucepot and sweat lightly. Cover vegetables with water and simmer on low for 30-35 mins.

❸ Remove broth from heat and strain through a fine mesh sieve. Pour over the tomato petals and vegetables from before. Simmer on low heat until vegetables are tender. Salt and pepper to taste.

❹ **Batter:** Put eggs, heavy cream and Parmesan cheese in blender and mix well. Pour into mixing bowl and add chopped herbs.

❺ **Fish:** Lightly dredge fish into seasoned flour, removing excess. Dip each filet into egg batter. Sauté in clarified butter or vegetable oil over medium heat for about 1 minute on each side, or until golden brown (medium doneness).

❻ To plate, divide the melted Roma tomato and vegetable stew into four bowls. Add your choice of starch at this time. Place fish filet on top of stew vegetables and garnish with chive sticks and nori (sushi paper) strips.

This is one of my favorite dishes, especially in the winter, because of its warming simplicity. You can substitute any milk-white fish, such as flounder filets or slices (about ½ inch thick) of grouper, snapper or even the famous Maryland rockfish. This dish can be served with freshly made pasta gnocchi and even steamed rice.

Photo: Annie Reid-Stone

Hampton's
CHEF NATE FINNEY

Grilled Swordfish Fillet

With Savory Swiss Chard, Plantain and Cannolini Bean Terrine With a Spicy Chiptole *Buerre Blanc* and Plantain Chips

Serves 6

6	8-oz. swordfish fillets
✓	salt & pepper
✓	oil for frying

Cannolini Bean Puree

1 TB.	cooking oil
4 cloves	garlic , peeled and chopped
2	shallots, peeled and chopped
1 TB.	white wine
1 can	cannolini beans

Terrine

2 heads	Swiss chard
2 unripe	plantains (green), sliced 1/8" thick
✓	Cannoli Bean puree (recipe above)

Chipolte Buerre Blanc

1 qt.	heavy cream
1 cup	white wine
1/2 cup	brown sugar
1 can	chipolte peppers, pureed
1 lb.	butter, cubed

❶Wash fillets and pat dry. Season with salt and pepper. Heat oil in sauté pan and sear fish until golden brown on both sides and cooked throughout.

❷**Bean Puree:** In a hot sauté pan, add oil, then garlic and shallots. When they are slightly browned, add white wine to deglaze pan. Add the can of beans. Let cook until liquid is reduced. Put mixture in blender and puree until smooth.

❸Preheat oven to 350°.

❹**Terrine:** Blanch Swiss chard in hot water for 1 minute; remove and shock in cold water. Use 6 triangular terrine molds (or any other shape), layer the Swiss chard on bottom, then place the sliced plantains along the sides, making a pocket. Put the Cannolini Bean Puree into the pocket; top with more plantains and more Swiss chard. Tuck sides in like a pie shell. Cover with aluminum foil and bake for 30 minutes.

❹Reduce heavy cream and white wine at a simmer for 8 minutes. Stir in brown sugar and pureed peppers. Remove from heat. Whisk in the cubed butter slowly. Strain and keep at room temperature.

❺To plate, place tureen on plate. Stack fish atop the tureen; put sauce over fish. Place 2 plantain chips over fish. Serve.

Photo courtesy of
Chiapparelli's Restaurant

Chiapparelli's Restaurant
CHEF RUSSEL FREW

Shrimp Nicola

Serves 2

12	jumbo shrimp
4 TB.	butter
2 tsp.	flour
✓	pinch salt
✓	pinch pepper
✓	pinch oregano
✓	pinch crushed red pepper
1 TB.	parsley, chopped
2 cloves	garlic, chopped
2 slices	lemon
3/4 cup	white wine
✓	garlic bread

❶ Peel and de-vein shrimp.

❷ Melt butter in a large saucepan over medium heat. Add shrimp; sauté until cooked through.

❸ Remove shrimp from pan and set aside.

❹ Whisk flour, seasonings, parsley, garlic into pan. Add lemon slices. Cook for 1 minute: garlic will be slightly browned.

❺ Add wine and whisk until combined. Cook for 1 minute longer.

❻ Add shrimp to sauce in pan and cook on medium heat until sauce has thickened and all alcohol has evaporated.

❼ Serve with garlic bread.

Photo courtesy of Restaurant “b”

Restaurant "b"
CHEF BRIAN GREENE

Maryland Rockfish with Oyster Stuffing

Serves 4

Stuffing

3 TB.	unsalted butter
3 oz.	Tasso ham, diced small
4 oz.	fine diced sweet onion
3 oz.	fine dice celery
3 oz.	fine dice red Bell pepper
3 oz.	scallion
2 TB.	chopped chive
8 oz.	shucked local oysters with liquor, roughly chopped
1 TB.	fresh thyme
1 tsp.	Tabasco sauce
2 TB.	Old Bay seasoning
4 oz.	bread crumbs

Fish

2 TB.	vegetable oil
4	5-oz. Wild Rockfish filets
2 tsp.	Kosher salt
✓	black pepper

❶**Stuffing:** Melt butter in a large sauté pan over medium heat. Add Tasso ham and diced vegetables. Cook until softened; add oysters (reserve their liquor).

❷Cook for 4 minutes, turning mixture often. Add remaining ingredients including reserved liquor from the oysters and cook for an additional 4 minutes, turning mixture often.

❸If stuffing is too dry or wet, adjust the amount of bread crumbs or add stock until you have the desired consistency.

❹Preheat oven to 350°.

❺**Fish Fillets:** Heat vegetable oil over medium high heat while seasoning the filets with Kosher salt and black pepper. When the oil is hot carefully place filets into pan, cooking one at a time until the surface of the meat is light golden brown.

❻Place filets skin side down on a non-stick baking pan and place the desired amount of stuffing on top of each filet. Put pan into a pre-heated oven. Cook for 14 minutes or until the stuffing is golden brown and the fish is firm to the touch.

❼Serve with a nice dry white wine and enjoy!

Photo: Annie Reid-Stone

Brighton's Orangerie
CHEF EDWIN "ZEUS" HERMAN

Grilled Freshwater Prawns with Caribbean Salsa

Serves 1

4	prawns, shelled
1	shallot, chopped
3 cloves	garlic, minced
✓	pinch salt and pepper
2 TB.	olive oil

Caribbean Salsa:

1/2	mango (ripe), diced small
1/2	avocado (ripe), diced small
3 oz.	pineapple (ripe), diced small
1	jalapeño (fresh), seeded and brunoise
1 TB.	cilantro, chopped
1 TB.	salt and pepper

Plating

1/2 cup	micro greens

❶ **Marinate Prawns:** Mix shallot, garlic, salt, pepper, and olive oil together to make a marinade. Marinate prawns for 1 hour.

❷ **Prepare Salsa:** Mix all ingredients in a bowl and let stand for 1 hour prior to serving.

❸ When prepared to serve, grill prawns over low heat for about 45 seconds on each side or until the prawns curl and turn a light pink.

❹ Place the salsa in a ring mold in the center of the plate and place the prawns around the salsa. Place micro greens on top.

Photo: Annie Reid-Stone

Shula's Steak House
CHEF TROY JONES

Shula's Signature Crabcake

Makes about 10

2 lbs.	lump crabmeat
2 lbs.	backfin crabmeat
1 oz.	Old Bay seasoning
1 oz.	chopped parsley
2 cups	sliced bread, cut into cubes
6	large eggs
1 cup	mayonnaise
2 oz.	Creole mustard
1 oz.	Worcestershire sauce
1 oz.	lemon juice

❶Drain crab meat; mix with Old Bay seasoning and parsley. Add fresh bread cubes. Mix together.

❷In a large mixing bowl, mix eggs, mayonnaise, mustard, Worcestershire sauce and lemon juice together.

❸Combine both mixtures until they are folded together.

❹Portion mixture into 8-ounce cakes.

❺In sauté pan, bring oil to a medium-high temperature; add crab cakes and sauté lightly on both sides until golden brown.

❻Serve with your favorite cocktail sauce. Enjoy!

Photo:
Annie Reid-Stone

Phillips Harborplace Restaurant
CHEF DENNIS MARCOUX

Seared Soft Shell Crabs

Summer Ragout, Fried Leeks & a White Raspberry Reduction

Serves 1

1	soft shell crab
✓	salt and pepper
1 cup	white balsamic vinegar
1/2 cup	red raspberries
1	plum tomato
1	shallot
2	leeks
1	zucchini
2 cups	white northern beans (drained)
1 tsp.	oil
1 cup	seafood stock

❶Dredge the crab in flour mixed with salt and pepper.

❷In a saucepan, reduce the white balsamic vinegar with red raspberries by half. Set aside to cool.

❸Cut plum tomato into half-inch chunks. Julienne shallot and white part of leeks. Set aside. Chop zucchini into half-inch dice.

❹In sauté pan, sauté shallots, half of the chopped leeks, zucchini and tomato until the tomato breaks down. Add beans and seafood stock; reduce until slightly thickened. Set aside. Season with salt and pepper.

❺Sauté the dredged soft shell crab in the oil for 3 minutes on each side. Toss remaining leeks in remaining seasoned flour mixture. Sauté in oil until crispy.

❻To assemble, cut the soft shell in half. Spoon ragout on plate, arrange soft shell crab on top, drizzle with balsamic reduction, and garnish with fried leeks.

Photo: Scott T. Mislan

Kali's Court

Chefs Brian Martin & Rashed Edwards

Monkfish Osso Bucco
with Seafood Cassoulet and Ratatouille

Serves 6

6	10-oz. Monkfish steaks (cut osso bucco style)
3 TB.	grapeseed oil, divided
✓	salt and pepper

Cassoulet

2 cups	cannelini beans
4	bacon strips
1	large white onion, divided
1	medium carrot, divided
2 stalks	celery, divided
4 cloves	garlic, crushed
1 bunch	thyme
1 1/2 qts.	light chicken stock
8 oz.	smoked haddie, cut in pieces
12	large shrimp, diced
1 TB.	finely chopped oregano, thyme and rosemary
1/4 cup	Panko (or as needed)
1 TB.	oil

Mussels

24	Mussels
1 tsp.	olive oil
1 cup	diced white onion
4 cloves	crushed garlic
1/4 cup	diced carrot
1/4 cup	diced celery
1 sprig	thyme
1/4 cup	white wine

❶**Preparing the Beans:** The day before, soak beans in water (at least 12 hours).

❷Drain and rinse the beans. In a saucepan, render bacon, and then add half the onion, half the carrot, 1 stalk of celery (each in large, rough cut), garlic and thyme.

❸When vegetables are soft, add beans and chicken stock. Simmer approximately 45 minutes or until beans are 2/3 of the way done.

❹Drain beans and spread on a pan to cool. While cooling, pick out all the vegetables, bacon and thyme.

❺**Mussels:** In a pot, heat 1 tablespoon oil and add the onions, garlic, carrot, celery and thyme.

❻Cook until soft and then add wine. Reduce by half and add mussels. Cover the mussels in water and simmer until the mussels have pulled to one side of the shell.

❼Pull mussels from pot and from shell. Put aside. Strain mussel broth and save.

Continued...

Photo: Scott T. Mislan

Kali's Court

CHEFS BRIAN MARTIN & RASHED EDWARDS

Monkfish Osso Bucco (continued)

Ratatouille

2 TB.	olive oil
1/2	red pepper, diced
1/2	white onion, diced
1 clove	garlic, minced
2	small zucchini, diced
1	small eggplant, diced
2	small tomatoes, skinned, seeded and diced
✓	salt and pepper

❶**Ratatouille:** Divide 2 tablespoons oil into 2 sauté pans. In one, sweat the red pepper. In the other, add the onions and garlic. Cook both until soft.

❷When onions are soft, add the eggplant and cook for 4 minutes.

❸Cool the vegetables and combine with other ingredients in a bowl. Season to taste.

❹Heat a sauté pan.Add grapeseed oil and monkfish seasoned with salt and pepper. Cook about 4 to 5 minutes on each side.

❺In the saucepan, add one tablespoon grapeseed oil, remaining half onion and carrot and remaining stalk celery (all diced). Cook until soft. Add beans and cover with mussel stock. Bring to a simmer. Add diced shrimp and smoked haddie, cook for 3 minutes.

❻To finish cassoulet, add the herbs, mussels and panko, until it thickens.

❼Heat another sauté pan and add last tablespoon grapeseed oil and ratatouille vegetables. Cook for 2 to 3 minutes.

❽**To Plate:** Spoon cassoulet mixture in the center of each plate. Encircle the beans with the ratatouille vegetables and place the monkfish on top of the beans.

Photo: Annie Reid-Stone

Grill 700

Chef Tim Mullen

Crab Crusted "George's Bank" Cod with Sweet Corn Butter Sauce

Serves 4

4	4-to-5 ounce cod fillets
1 TB.	mayonnaise
1	egg
2 tsp.	Old Bay seasoning
1 tsp.	dry mustard
1/2 tsp.	baking powder
6 dashes	Worcestershire Sauce
✓	few dashes hot sauce
1 tsp.	minced chives
1 slice	white bread, crust removed, very small dice
6 oz.	crabmeat

Corn Butter Sauce

2 ears	corn on the cob
2 tsp.	olive oil, divided
1 tsp.	butter
2	shallots, small dice
1 TB.	flour
6 oz.	Half and Half
2 oz.	white wine (Chardonnay)
✓	salt and pepper (optional)

❶Preheat oven to 400°.

❷Wash and pat dry the cod filets.

❸In large mixing bowl, combine mayonnaise, egg, Old Bay, mustard, baking powder, Worcestershire Sauce, hot sauce and chives. Mix until well blended.

❹Add diced bread; fold in crab meat.

❺Divide this mixture between the four fish filets, topping each one and spreading evenly.

❻Bake fish for 15 mins., or until golden brown.

❼**Sauce:** Shuck and remove silk from corn. Rub ears lightly with one teaspoon olive oil, wrap in foil to make a pouch and bake in 400° oven for 20 minutes until kernels are soft.

❽Take out of oven; let cool; remove kernels and set aside.

❾In a sauce pan, sauté shallots in a teaspoon of oil and butter until soft. Add flour, stirring over medium heat for a few minutes. Flour should absorb all of the butter. Whisk in white wine, Half and Half, and corn kernels. Simmer for 8 to 10 minutes.

❿Puree in a blender until smooth, strain, season to taste.

Continued...

Photo: Annie Reid-Stone

Grill 700
CHEF TIM MULLEN

Crab Crusted Cod (continued)

Serves 4

Tomato Oil

4	Roma tomatoes
1/2 cup	olive oil
1 TB.	tomato paste
1/3 cup	white vinegar
✓	pinch Grey or Sea salt

❶ Cut tomatoes in half; squeeze out as much liquid as possible. Rub lightly with some of the olive oil and roast in 400° oven until soft and lightly browned in color, 25 to 30 minutes.

❷ Add tomato paste to the tomatoes, mix together and roast another 5 minutes. Cool.

❸ When cool, puree the mixture in a blender or food processor, adding all remaining oil and the vinegar. Season to taste; set aside.

❹ **To serve:** Place fish fillets in center of plate. Spoon corn sauce around fish and drizzle a little tomato oil on sauce. Serve with your favorite fresh seasonal vegetables. Enjoy!

Photo:
Annie Reid-Stone

Grill 700

CHEF TIM MULLEN

Chilled Jumbo Shrimp

Caramelized Tomato Tart & Horseradish Pepper Sauce

Serves 1

5	jumbo shrimp (size 16/20")
2	lemons, cut in half
1	lime, cut in half
2 oz.	pickling spice
3	fresh asparagus spears
1 TB.	shaved Parmesan cheese
✓	micro greens for garnish

Tomato Tart

1	puff pastry shell (sold frozen)
1	egg, beaten
3 to 4	roasted tomatoes* (Roma tomatoes work well)
✓	Extra virgin olive oil
✓	Sea salt

Horseradish Pepper Sauce

1	6-oz. jar of roasted red peppers
1 TB.	grated horseradish

❶ Blanch shrimp in simmering water with lemon and lime halves and pickling spice. Remove from heat and cool immediately in an ice bath. Remove from water and refrigerate until ready to serve.

❷ **Tomato Tart:** Preheat oven to 350°. Cut a 3-inch circle from the puff pastry. Brush with beaten egg and bake for 12 to 15 minutes until golden brown.

❸ Reduce oven to 225° and bake for another 20-30 minutes until dough is cooked throughout.

❹ When pastry is done, remove from oven and use a spatula to transfer to a plate.

❺ Cook asparagus by grilling it until tender.

❻ **Horseradish sauce:** Remove skin from all peppers and blend with horseradish. Puree.

❼ To assemble, place half of the cheese on pre-baked puff pastry and top with roasted tomatoes then the other half of the cheese. Place in a 325° oven until nicely warmed.

❽ To serve, place asparagus on plate with warmed tart on top and a small mound of tossed greens next to it. Place 5 chilled shrimp next to the greens and the pepper sauce next to the shrimp. Enjoy!

* *To roast tomatoes, cut tomatoes in half lengthwise. Season very lightly with extra virgin olive oil and sea salt. Roast in 225° oven for a few hours until tomatoes are tender and approximately half their size. (It is better to do a large batch of 12 to 24 tomatoes; they can be held in an air tight container in a refrigerator, covered in extra virgin olive oil. They can be used in pastas, salads or as an appetizer on baguette slices or crisps.)*

Photo courtesy of Brewer's Art

CHEF RAVI NARAYANAN

Black Pepper Encrusted Rockfish

with Tomato & Roasted Garlic Grits, wilted Mustard Greens and Yellow Tomato Fumet

Serves 4

1	whole rockfish, filleted
2	onions, rough chop
2	celery stalks, rough chop
4	yellow tomatoes, medium, diced
3	bay leaves
1 TB.	whole black pepper
3 oz.	butter, divided
1 cup	white wine
✓	salt and pepper to taste
1 cup	grits, dry measure
1 cup	heavy cream
1 clove	garlic, roasted and mashed
1/2 lb.	mustard greens, washed and dried
2 TB.	cooking oil

❶ **Fish:** Scale and fillet the fish with the skin on and reserve bones along with the head and tail. Most fishmongers will do this for you if you ask. Portion the fillets into 4 equal portions and score the skin to prevent the fish fillet from curling as they are being cooked. Reserve until later.

❷ In a heavy stockpot, sauté onions, celery, 3 yellow tomatoes, bay leaf and black pepper in 2 ounces of butter. Add the fish bones along with the head and tail. Add the white wine and fill pot with water until fish is covered. Bring to a slow simmer and cook 1 1/2 hours; strain and reserve the liquid. Salt and pepper to taste.

❸ **Grits:** Follow package directions, substituting 1 cup of heavy cream for one cup of water. Add the garlic, remaining yellow tomato, and remaining ounce of butter. Cook on low heat until the grits are tender and creamy. Salt and pepper to taste. Reserve until ready to serve.

❹ **Service:** Preheat oven to 375°. Bring the fish fumet to a boil in a pot or sauté pan. Heat the grits in a pan or in the oven. On the flesh side of the fish, generously grind fresh black pepper, coating the fish. Heat a large sauté pan to very hot. Add the cooking oil to the pan and place the fish fillets in the pan skin side down. Cook on each side approximately 3 to 4 minutes and finish in a 375° oven.

❺ In a large bowl, portion the grits into four equal parts. Place the fish on top of the grits. Using the sauté pan the fish was cooked in, wilt the mustard greens and place on top of the fish. Pour 4 equal portions of the fish fumet into each bowl. Serve immediately.

It is best to use course ground grits or stone ground grits. I use stone ground grits from Falls Mill in Belevedere, TN. You can get them online at www.fallsmill.com

Photo: Annie Reid-Stone

Window's Restaurant, Renaissance Harborplace Hotel

CHEF FELIX NUÑEZ

Lobster Burgers

Makes 3

4 oz.	lobster meat (1 claw; half of a tail)
3	mini brioche
✓	Banana leaf (cut to size of plate)
3 TB.	Tarragon Aioli (see below)
1/2	avocado, sliced
1 oz.	mixed micro greens

Tarragon Aioli

5	egg yolks
1 TB.	Dijon Mustard
2 cups	salad oil
1 bunch	chopped tarragon
✓	salt and pepper to taste
✓	Juice of 1/2 lemon

Lotus Root Chips

✓	lotus root
✓	salt
✓	cumin

❶Heat lobster meat in a bur Monte sauce (which is whole butter warmed up slowly; usually started with a base of water and held at a medium temperature to prevent breakage).

❷**Prepare Tarragon Aioli:** Place egg yolks and Dijon mustard in a blender. Once blended, slowly start to add salad oil (place salad oil in a bottle and squeeze out gently). Once all oil is added, add tarragon, then season with salt and pepper. Fold In lemon juice. Aioli should hold for 3 to 4 days.

❸**Prepare Lotus Root Chips:** Peel pieces of lotus root paper thin. Deep fry; drain; dust with salt & cumin.

❹Slice brioche in half and toast.

❺Place banana leaf on the plate. Place Lotus Root chips in bowl on plate.

❻Drizzle aioli on bottom half of each toasted brioche.

❼Put a slice of avocado atop aioli.

❽Place lobster meat atop avocado; garnish with mixed micro greens. Put top of brioche atop burgers and place on plate and serve.

Vin Restaurant

Chef Chris Patternote

Slow Poached Swordfish

Serves 2

2	tomatoes
5	sprigs Italian parsley
10	spears chives
3	sprigs tarragon
3	sprigs thyme
✓	salt and pepper to taste
5 cups	high quality olive oil
10	Kalamata olives
10	pieces baby zucchini
2	6-oz. pieces center cut swordfish (trimmed of skin and blood line)
✓	cooking oil

❶ Preheat oven to 425°.

❷ With sharp knife, make a small "x" in bottom of each tomato. Dip them in boiling water for 15 seconds, then plunge into ice bath. Skin will easily peel off.

❸ Quarter the tomatoes and squeeze out seeds. Set aside.

❹ Pick herbs off stems, chop roughly, and mix together. Set stems aside for later.

❺ Toss tomatoes with pinch of salt and pepper, pinch of herbs and lightly coat with olive oil. Spread on a sheet pan and bake for 20 minutes or until lightly brown and wrinkled.

❻ Remove seeds from olives and julienne them (cut into strips).

❼ Trim stem off zucchini and slice lengthwise in half. On medium heat, sauté in olive oil skin side up until lightly brown. Flip over and finish cooking. Skin should remain bright green. Season with salt and pepper.

❽ In saucepan, heat oil to 195-200°. Season fish with salt and pepper and carefully place swordfish filets into oil (do not drop in). Fish must be submerged in oil. To achieve this easily, lay fish in gently with a spatula.

❾ Leave pot uncovered while cooking. Fish will take approximately 15-20 minutes to be fully cooked. You can tell it's done when you see small white "beads" on the fish. This is the fat trying to escape. Then, remove pot from heat but let fish rest in oil until ready to serve.

Continued...

Vin Restaurant
Chef Chris Patternote

Slow Poached Swordfish (continued)

Port Reduction

1 liter	bottle Tanney Port
1 liter	bottle Cabernet Redux
✓	parsley stems (from earlier)
✓	thyme stems (from earlier)
✓	tarragon stems (from earlier)
1	bay leaf
5	peppercorns

❶ Put Port reduction ingredients into heavy bottom pot and on medium heat, reduce until reduction begins to foam heavily. (About 2½ cups of reduction.)

❷ **Prepare Sauce:** Use 2 ounces of the cooking oil and 1 ounce of the reduction, olives and a large pinch of herbs. In a bowl, simply mix all this together with a spoon. Do not over-stir; sauce should be separated.

❸ Begin plating the swordfish by placing zucchini side by side on center of plate.

❹ Carefully remove fish from oil using slotted spatula and place on top of zucchini. Arrange tomatoes on top of fish.

❺ Spoon sauce around plate, making sure there is no extra liquid on plate or your port reduction will run. Serve.

Sabatino's Italian Restaurant
CHEF RENATO ROTONDO, SR.

Shrimp Renato

Serves 4

12	slices prosciutto (thin)
12	slices mozzarella cheese (thin)
24	jumbo shrimp
1/2 cup	lemon juice
1/2 lb.	melted butter
✓	salt and pepper to taste
1/4 tsp.	oregano
✓	dash Accent
1/4 cup	brandy
1/4 cup	sweet white wine
3 cups	cooked white rice

❶Cut prosciutto and mozzarella into pieces approximately the size of your shrimp.

❷Peel shrimp, but leave the tails on. De-vein and slice underside lengthwise almost to vein, leaving "hinge" intact. Spread open and flatten to form a butterfly shape. Place butterflied shrimp in broiler pan.

❸Mix together lemon juice and melted butter and pour over shrimp. Season with salt, pepper, oregano and Accent.

❹Broil shrimp on both sides until they are pink and no longer clear. Remove from broiler.

❹Combine brandy and wine.

❺Place a piece of prosciutto and a piece of mozzarella cheese over each shrimp. Pour the brandy wine mixture over the shrimp. Return to broiler until cheese is melted.

❻Carefully spoon 6 shrimp over rice (preferably in a bowl) and pour brandy wine mixture over top.

Photo: Annie Reid-Stone

Tío Pepe Restaurant
CHEF EMILIO SANZ

Paella Valenciana

Serves 4

1/2 cup	olive oil
1	whole chicken, cut into 8 pieces
1/2 lb.	veal, cut into cubes
2 cloves	garlic, minced
1	onion, chopped
1	fresh red pepper, chopped
1	squid, cleaned and sliced
2 cups	uncooked rice
5 cups	chicken broth or water
✓	pinch of saffron
1/2 cup	green peas
1/2 cup	string beans
1 lb.	shrimp
12	mussels
8	clams
1/2	whole lobster, cut into pieces
5	canned red pimientos, sliced into 1-inch thick pieces
✓	salt to taste
✓	fresh lemon for garnish

❶ Preheat oven to 450°.

❷ In a paella pan, heat the olive oil over a high flame. Add the chicken pieces and veal cubes, allow to brown.

❸ Next, add the garlic, onion, fresh red pepper, and squid. Cook, stirring ingredients until all are slightly browned.

❹ Then add the rice, combining it with the other ingredients. Add the chicken broth (or water) and saffron. Heat to boiling. Then add green beans and green peas. Allow to cook.

❺ Next, add shrimp, mussels, clams and lobster. Allow to boil, add the sliced pimientos, arranged on top of other ingredients.

❻ Remove from stovetop and place in preheated oven for 25 minutes.

❼ Adjust seasoning and serve with fresh lemon.

Photo courtesy of Crossroads Restaurant

Crossroads Restaurant at Radisson Cross Keys
CHEF TOM SCHWARZWELLER

Chesapeake Seafood Stew

Serves 1

4	Littleneck clams
4 oz.	clam broth
2 oz.	white wine
1/2 tsp.	garlic, chopped
✓	pinch saffron threads
3 oz.	Marinara or tomato sauce
1 oz.	jumbo lump crab meat
4	shrimp (10/15 count)
4	scallops
2 oz.	Rockfish in 2" square pieces
4	new red potatoes quarters, blanched
8	asparagus spears, blanched
✓	Old Bay seafood seasoning, to taste
✓	Fresh parsley, chopped

❶Combine the clams, broth, wine, garlic and saffron in a sauté pan, covered the pan to bring it up to full heat and cook until the clams start opening.

❷Add the marinara sauce and the rest of the seafood. Cook until the seafood is cooked through, about 7 minutes.

❸While that is cooking, heat the potatoes and asparagus in boiling water.

❹To serve, arrange the asparagus in a pasta bowl. Add the potatoes to the seafood, adjust the seasonings to your taste and pour into the bowl. Top with crab meat and sprinkle with the parsley.

This is a very simple recipe using many ingredients from our Bay.

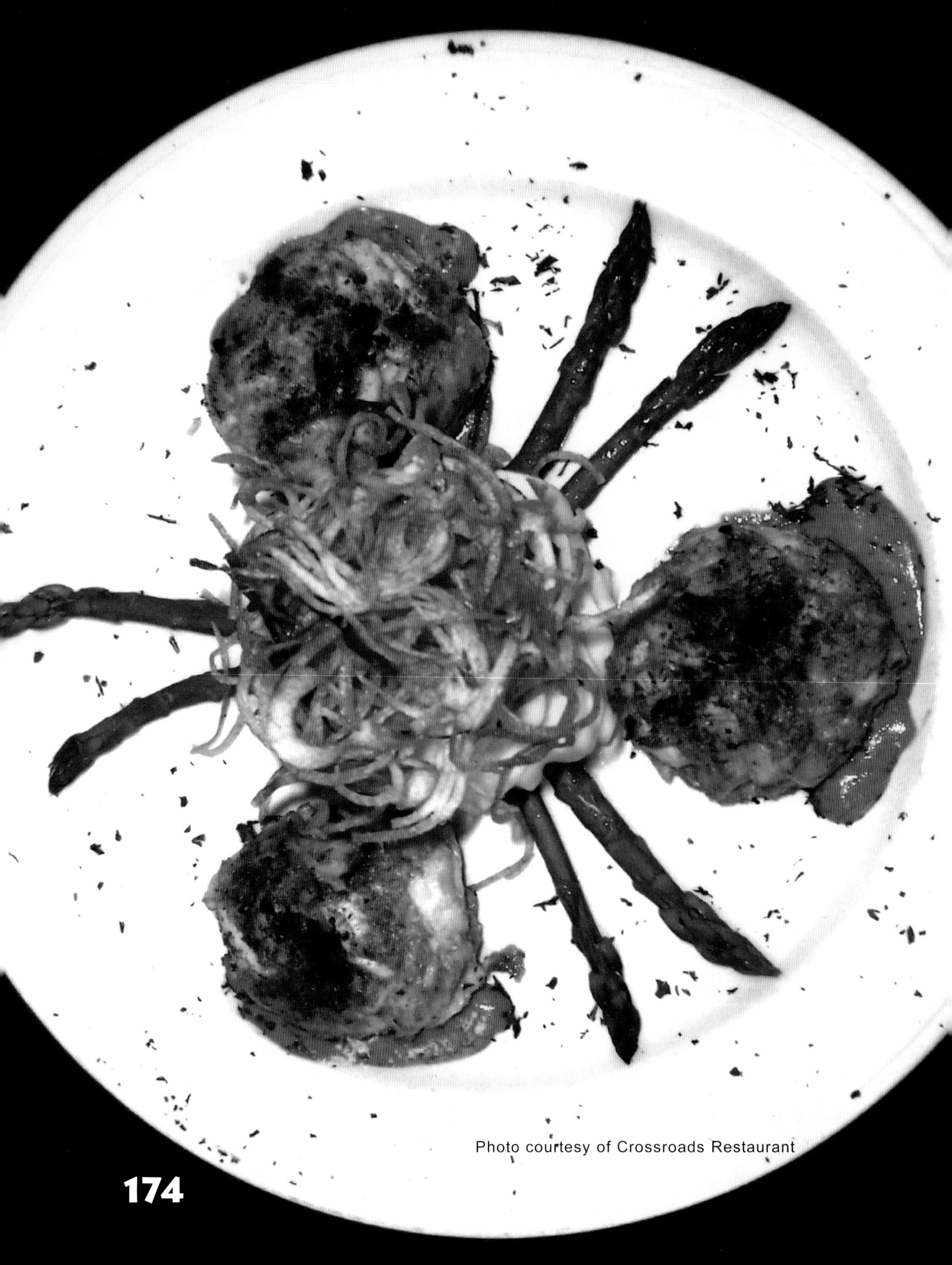

Photo courtesy of Crossroads Restaurant

Crossroads Restaurant at Radisson Cross Keys
CHEF TOM SCHWARZWELLER

Crab Cakes

Serves 2

1 lb.	jumbo lump crab meat, picked
1/2 cup	mayonnaise
1	egg
1/2 tsp.	Old Bay seasoning
✓	juice of one lemon
1/4 tsp.	dry ground mustard
1 TB.	Worcestershire sauce
1 cup	dry bread crumbs, unflavored
1/3 cup	fresh parsley, chopped
6	asparagus spears, blanched
4 oz.	mashed potatoes

Roasted Garlic Aioli

24	garlic cloves, peeled
✓	olive oil
✓	Kosher salt and fresh black pepper
4 cups	mayonnaise
4 tsp.	Dijon mustard
2	lemons, juiced
1 TB.	fresh parsley, chopped

❶ Combine all ingredients (except asparagus and potatoes) in a bowl. Mix well, adjusting seasonings and consistency.

❷ Make 3 ounce balls and place on broiler pan.

❸ Broil until golden brown and hot throughout, approximately 10 to 12 minutes.

❹ Preheat oven to 325°.

❺ **Roasted Garlic Aioli:** Roast the garlic cloves by lying the peeled cloves on a cookie sheet with a lip, drizzle with olive oil and season with salt and pepper. Add just enough water to cover the bottom of the pan.

❻ Cover with foil and bake at 325° for 30 to 45 minutes, or until very tender. (Watch the timing very closely).

❼ Remove garlic from pan and allow to cool.

❽ When garlic is roasted, combine the remaining ingredients in a blender and blend smooth. Add lemon juice if consistency is too thick.

These were voted Baltimore's best crabcakes by the City Paper, 2000.

❾ **To serve:** Pour the aioli on to a plate and fan it out. Arrange the asparagus into a peace symbol in groups of 2. Place the crab cakes in between the asparagus, with the mashed potatoes in the center of the plate. Sprinkle with chopped parsley.

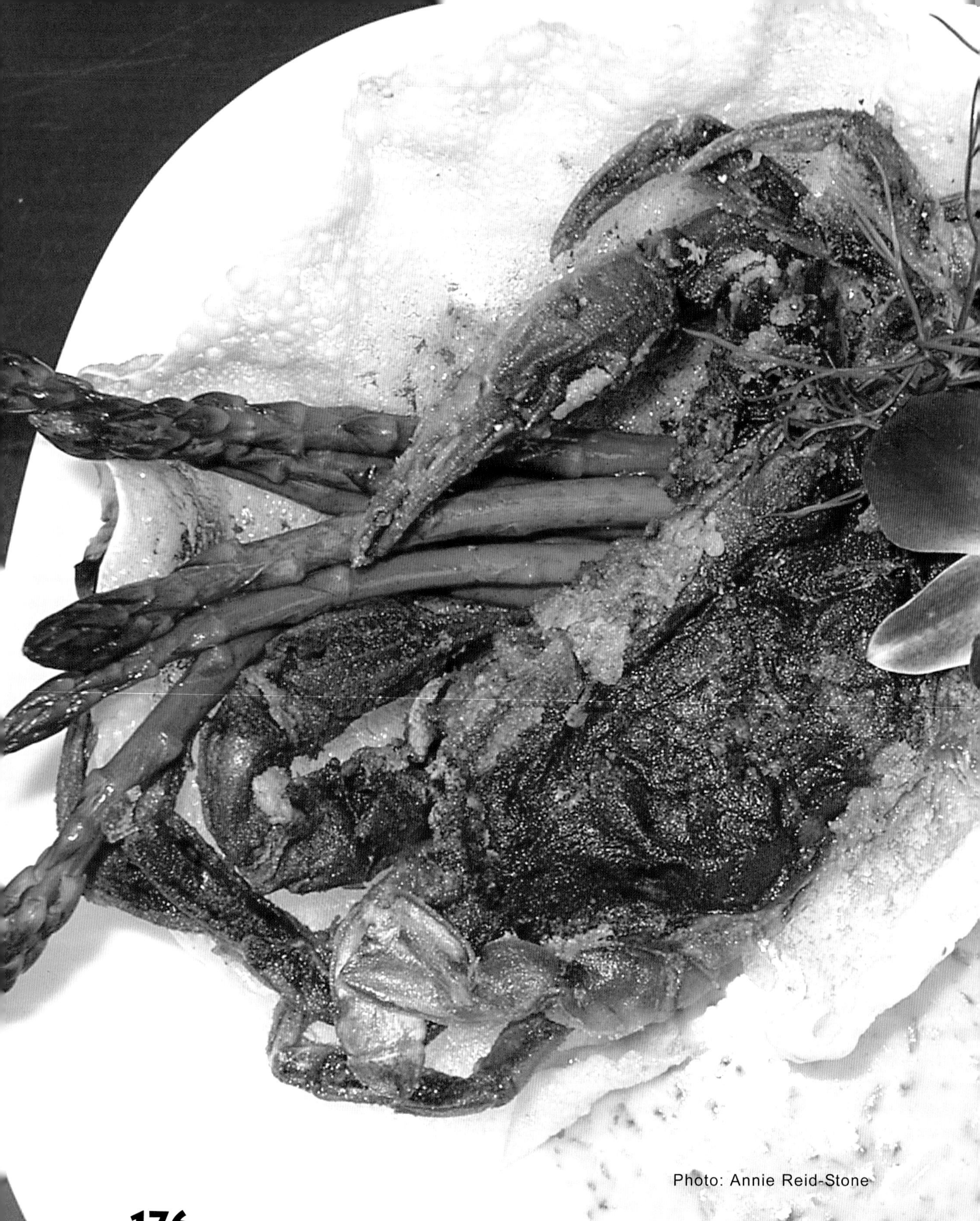

Photo: Annie Reid-Stone

Gertrude's
CHEF JOHN SHIELDS

Baltimore-Style Busters Bernaise

Serves 4

1 cup	flour
2 tsp.	Chesapeake seafood seasoning
1/2 tsp.	salt
1/2 tsp.	freshly ground black pepper
1/4 tsp.	cayenne, or to taste
8	soft shelled crabs, primes or jumbos, cleaned
4 TB.	butter (1/2 stick)
2 TB.	olive oil
✓	juice of 1 lemon
2 TB.	chopped fresh parsley

Bernaise Sauce

3 TB.	dry white wine
2 TB.	white wine vinegar
1 TB.	Minced shallots
1 tsp.	minced fresh tarragon leaves
1/4 tsp.	freshly ground black pepper
1/8 tsp.	salt
3	egg yolks
2 TB.	boiling water
8 TB.	butter, melted (1 stick)
2 TB.	fresh chopped parsley or tarragon leaves

❶Stir together the flour, seafood seasoning, salt, pepper and cayenne in bowl. Dredge the soft shells lightly in the mixture, shaking off excess.

❷In large skillet over medium high heat, warm the butter and oil. Add soft shells and sauté for 3 mins on each side. Remove and keep warm. Pour off half the cooking oil and return the pan to heat. Add the lemon juice and parsley. Heat for 1 minute, and then pour over crabs.

❸**Sauce:** In small saucepan, combine the first 6 ingredients. Bring to a boil and reduce to 1 tablespoon. Set aside to cool.

❹In the top of a double boiler, place egg yolks, tarragon reduction, and the boiling water. Place over barely simmering water and whisk together until mixture becomes pale and creamy.

❺Remove from the heat and gradually whisk in the melted butter to make a thick sauce. (This works best if the butter and the egg mixture are the same temperature.) When thickened, gently whisk in the parsley or tarragon.

❻Serve crabs topped with a dollop of Bernaise sauce.

Traditionally, this dish was made with busters, the very tiny soft shell crabs that are actually no longer harvested. But it's the perfect preparation for any soft-shelled crabs. Ask at the fish market for primes or jumbos (also called hotels). Bernaise sauce, which is basically hollandaise with an herb reduction added, is lovely paired with sautéed soft-shell crabs, but you can use other piquant sauces as well.

Photo courtesy of Red Fish

Red Fish

CHEF TED STELZENMULLER

Pan Seared Salmon with Saffron Seafood Sauce

Serves 6

Seafood

6	8-oz. salmon fillets
3 TB.	canola or vegetable oil for frying

Sauce

1 TB.	olive oil
1 tsp.	garlic, chopped
1/4 cup	white wine
1 TB.	sun-dried tomatoes
1/4 cup	seafood broth or stock
✓	pinch of saffron
1 tsp.	lemon zest
✓	pinch of pepper

Sweet Potato Hay

1	sweet potato, small
✓	vegetable oil for frying
✓	salt and pepper to taste

❶Rinse the salmon gently in cool water and pat it dry with a paper towel.

❷On high heat, in a non-stick pan, add the oil until it smokes. Add the salmon to the pan and sauté for 5 minutes. When the fish is golden brown, flip it over and finish for another 4 to 5 minutes. Remove and keep warm.

❸**Sauce:** Heat olive oil over medium heat; add chopped garlic and sauté for 1 minute. Add the white wine and reduce by half. Add the tomatoes, seafood broth, saffron and lemon zest. Bring the sauce to a boil and season with a pinch of pepper. As soon as it comes to a boil, remove pan from heat.

❹**Sweet potato hay:** Peel the sweet potato and cut it into match stick pieces.

❺In a small pot, heat vegetable oil over medium high heat. When the oil is hot, add the sweet potato and fry until it just starts to turn a shade darker. Pull it out and form it into a ball. Salt and pepper to taste.

❻Serve salmon with sauce and top with sweet potato hay.

The crisp texture from searing brings out the natural sweetness of salmon. This is also a great low fat flavorful dish. Just leave off the sweet potato hay.

Photo courtesy of Red Fish

Red Fish

Rockfish Rochelle

Serves 6

Seafood

6	8-oz. skin-on Rockfish filets
✓	canola or vegetable oil
✓	salt and pepper to taste

Sauce

1	small shallot, diced
✓	oil for frying
1/2 cup	heavy whipping cream
1 tsp.	fresh thyme
2 TB.	butter
2 to 3 oz.	Maryland crabmeat
✓	salt and pepper

❶ Rinse the Rockfish gently in cool water, and pat dry with a paper towel. Score the skin of the Rockfish so it stays flat in the pan.

❷ Heat canola or vegetable oil in a non-stick pan until it smokes. Add the fish, skin side down, and turn down the heat to medium. Salt and pepper the fish to taste.

❸ Don't touch the fish for 4 minutes. The skin should be golden brown. Flip it over and finish cooking for another 4 to 5 minutes. Keep warm.

❹ **Sauce:** Over medium low heat, brown the shallots in a small amount of oil. Add heavy cream and reduce by half.

❺ Add the fresh thyme and whisk in the cold butter vigorously.

❻ Add the crabmeat and salt and pepper to taste.

❼ To serve, plate the Rockfish and serve with the sauc

This is a version of one of my most popular dishes. The rich yet neutral flavors work great with almost any side dish. I love this dish so much it will always be on my menu.

CHEF BRYAN SULLIVAN

Shrimp, Crab & Lobster Tart

Serves 4-6

Tart Dough for Shell

5 cups	all purpose flour
3 sticks	unsalted butter,chilled
1 tsp.	salt
4	eggs, slightly beaten

Tart Mix

1/4 cup	heavy cream
1/8 cup	white wine
✓	juice of half a lemon
2	whole eggs
1 cup	mayonnaise
1 TB.	chopped parsley
1 tsp.	Old Bay seasoning
✓	pinch of cayenne pepper
✓	pinch nutmeg
✓	salt & pepper

Seafood

6 ozs.	cooked lobster meat, cut into bite-sized pieces
1/2 lb.	shrimp (21/25 size), cut into 3 pieces each
1/2 lb.	jumbo lump crab meat
✓	salt and pepper to taste

❶**Tart Shell:** Put flour and chilled butter into electric paddle mixer; mix until the butter is blended into the flour (resembling crumbs). Add salt and eggs. Mix until dough comes together, but finish by hand. Cover with waxed paper and refrigerate for 2 hours.

❷Preheat oven to 350º.

❸Roll out dough to 1/8" thickness. Cut into pieces large enough to fit into your tart pans. Mold into individual tart shells. Crumble a piece of wax paper to make it soft, place on top of dough and fill with beans. The paper keeps the beans out of the dough, and the beans keep the dough from rising.

❹Bake for 8-12 minutes or until edges become slightly brown. When cool, remove beans and wax paper.

❺**Tart Mix:** Mix the cream, wine, lemon juice, egg, mayonnaise, parsley, Old Bay seasoning, cayenne and nutmeg together. Whip with a whisk a few times and finish with salt and pepper. The mixture will give the tart flavor and texture.

❻Bring oven to 375º. Place the seafood in a bowl; add just enough tart mix to make it wet and slightly creamy. Season with salt and pepper. Spoon the mix into pre-baked tart shells. Bake for 8-10 minutes. Remove from the oven when slightly brown.

❼Serve with olive oil and balsamic vinegar, or with a mixed green salad.

This tart is great for a first course, as a lunch entrée or a main course for dinner.

Photo: Annie Reid-Stone

Abacrombie Fine Foods & Accommodations

CHEF SONNY SWEETMAN

Maryland Chesapeake Bay Rockfish in Puff Pastry

Serves 4

Crepes

2 bunches	parsley
6 oz.	milk
1 1/2 tsp.	extra virgin olive oil
1/2 tsp.	salt
1/2 tsp.	green curry paste
2 oz.	egg, lightly beaten (about 1 1/2)
2 oz.	flour (1 bread and 1 cake) or all purpose flour

Braised Cabbage

1/4 head	Savoy cabbage
1	Gala apple, fine diced
1/4	onion
4 strips	bacon
1/4 cup	cream
1/4 tsp.	ground coriander
✓	salt and pepper
✓	butter

Final Preparation

1 sheet	puff pastry dough
4	6-oz. portions Rockfish, boneless and skinless filets
1	whole egg for egg wash

❶ **Crepes:** Place cleaned parsley in blender. Add milk and puree until green in color. Add olive oil, salt, and green curry paste and pulse the machine. Add eggs and flour and pulse again.

❷ Warm a non-stick pan and pour 2 ounces of the mix in a thin layer in the pan. When cooked through (approximately 2 minutes on medium heat), take out of pan and let cool. Repeat.

❸ **Cabbage:** Cut cabbage in thin ribbons. Dice the apple, bacon and onions into small pieces. Render the bacon in a cast iron pan and immediately add apple and onion. When they are translucent in color, add the cream, coriander and cabbage. Finish with salt pepper and butter.

❹ Preheat oven to 400°.

❺ **Final Preparation:** Cut the puff pastry dough into lattice. Lay the crepe on the inside of the puff pastry dough. Place 2 tablespoons of cooled braised cabbage on the crepe. Season one portion of the rockfish fillet; lay on the cabbage and roll pastry forward as if you were making an apple strudel or a spring roll. The dough should meet on the bottom of the fish. Do this four times; brush the outside with egg wash and bake for 12 to 15 minutes, until golden brown. Serve hot.

This recipe was selected as Best Usage of Seafood from the Chesapeake Bay at the Maryland Seafood Challenge.

Chef Graham Weber

Chesapeake Harvest

Serves 4

Grits	
4 oz.	maple pepper bacon, julienne
22 oz.	chicken stock
4 oz.	grits
2 ears	corn, grilled and shucked

❶**Grits:** In a small saucepan over moderate heat, render bacon until crisp. Add chicken stock and bring to a boil. Whisk in grits and continue to mix for a minute. Reduce heat and let simmer for 20 minutes. Add corn and keep warm.

Vegetables	
4 oz.	olive oil, divided
4 oz.	baby spinach
1 oz.	garlic, minced
✓	salt and pepper
12	Heirloom tomatoes cut in ⅓-inch slices
1 tsp.	basil

❷**Vegetables:** In a sauté pan over moderate heat, add a splash of olive oil, spinach and garlic. Toss just until spinach starts to wilt. Season with salt and pepper. In a side bowl, toss the tomato slices with some olive oil, garlic and basil. Grill on each side for one minute.

Sauce:	
6 oz.	butter, at room temp.
8 oz.	rock shrimp
4 oz.	shallots, minced
4 oz.	Cognac
1 pint	shrimp stock
1	Bay leaf
1 oz.	chervil
✓	salt and pepper to taste

❸**Sauce:** In a saucepot over medium heat, add 1 ounce of butter and sauté shrimp until cooked through. Remove shrimp and set aside. Add shallots and cook until translucent. Next, add cognac and reduce by half. Add shrimp stock and bay leaf and reduce by half again. Turn off heat and whisk in butter, shrimp, and chervil. Season with salt and pepper to taste.

Continued...

Chesapeake Harvest (continued)

Fish:

4	Rockfish fillets, 4-oz. each
✓	oil for frying
✓	salt and pepper to taste
1 tsp.	garlic
1 tsp.	thyme

Crab:

4	soft shell crabs, cut in half
4 oz.	flour, seasoned with Old Bay
✓	chives, chopped
4 sprigs	chervil
1 oz.	chervil oil

❹**Fish:** Season with salt, pepper, garlic, and thyme and sear in a sauté pan over high heat until golden brown and cooked through.

❺**Crab:** Dredge in seasoned flour and sauté in small pan with some oil until crisp on both sides.

❻**Assembly:** Spoon 4 ounces of grits on each plate. Next, add 1 ounce of sautéed spinach directly on top of grits, followed by a grilled tomato slice, then half a crab, tomato, rockfish, tomato, crab and finish with a sprig of chervil.

❼Spoon sauce around the entrée and drizzle with chervil oil. Serve.

Photo: Annie Reid-Stone

Charleston
Chef Cindy Wolf

Sea Scallop BLT

Sauteed Sea Scallops with Smoked Applewood Bacon, Ripe Yellow Tomato and Baby Arugula

Serves 4

8 strips	Applewood smoked bacon (or thick-cut smoked bacon)
1	small shallot, finely diced
1/4 cup	fresh squeezed lemon juice
10 tsp.	extra virgin olive oil, divided
✓	salt and pepper
20	sea scallops, large (U-10)
2 bunches	baby arugula, rinsed and dried
4	ripe yellow tomatoes, large, cut into 5 slices each
✓	fresh herbs (chives, basil, oregano, etc.)

❶Cook bacon until crisp. Remove from pan, drain grease.

❷In a small bowl, whisk together shallot, lemon juice, and 4 teaspoons olive oil. Add salt and pepper to taste.

❸Heat a non-stick pan. Add 2-3 teaspoons olive oil. Carefully place half of the scallops in pan so that they are not overcrowded.

❹Brown on both sides (insides of scallops will be medium-rare to medium). Remove, keep warm. Continue for remaining scallops.

❺Arrange bed of arugula on plate. Add in layers of sliced tomatoes, bacon and scallops.

❻Add fresh herbs to lemon juice mixture.

❼Finish plates with a drizzle of lemon dressing and garnish with fresh herbs or flowers.

Photo:
Annie Reid-Stone

Baldwin's Station
CHEF ERIC YEAGER

Hawaiian Butter Fish

with Cherry Tomato Cream Sauce & Sweet Potato Mash

Serves 4

4	sweet potatoes, large chop
2	Yukon Gold potatoes, large chop
4 oz.	butter
2 oz.	orange juice
1 tsp.	nutmeg
2 oz.	honey
✓	salt & pepper
2 cups	heavy cream
½ pint	cherry tomatoes, sliced in half
2 cloves	garlic
✓	olive oil
✓	salt and pepper to taste
2 cups	heavy cream
1 tsp.	paprika
✓	butter
✓	salt and pepper
4	Hawaiian Butter Fish, 6-oz. portions
2 oz.	vegetable oil
✓	salt, pepper, and garlic to taste
1 bunch	asparagus

❶ Set a pot of water on stove and bring to a boil. Peel and rinse sweet potatoes and Yukon gold potatoes. Carefully place the potatoes in water. Cook until tender (do not overcook). Remove from water and place into a large bowl.

❷ Add butter, orange juice, nutmeg and honey to the potatoes and mash until smooth. Fold in the heavy cream and season to taste. Move mixture to bowl, and cover to keep warm.

❸ For the cherry tomato sauce, sauté cherry tomato halves in a sauce pot with a little oil, salt, pepper, and garlic. When tomatoes have cooked down, add cream and reduce. Add paprika. Season with salt and pepper to taste.

❹ Pre-heat oven to 350°.

❺ On medium high heat, warm a sauté pan on stove with 2 ounces vegetable oil. Season the fish with salt, pepper, and garlic. When the pan is hot, add fish. Cook on each side for 3 minutes, then place fish in an oven-proof container and put it in the oven. Cook for 5 minutes.

❻ Cut asparagus straight down to form halves. Sauté with a little butter, salt, and pepper.

❼ To serve, place sweet potatoes in the middle of the plate. Place fish on top of the sweet potatoes. Place asparagus on top of the fish. Drizzle sauce around the plate.

This recipe offers a beautiful palette and allows for an artistic presentation. Be creative!

Photo: Annie Reid-Stone

Intercontinental Harbor Court Hotel
Chef Joshua Young

Bacon Wrapped Sea Scallops with Truffle Cream Corn & Leeks

Serves 1

4	sea scallops, Jumbo (U-10) dry pack
4 slices	bacon
4	toothpicks
✓	salt and pepper

Truffle Cream Corn

2 ears	fresh sweet corn with the kernels taken off the cob
1	leek cut in 1/2 moons (washed and dried)
1 cup	heavy cream
✓	salt and pepper to taste

To plate

6 leaves	arugula
✓	juice of 1/2 fresh lemon
✓	extra-virgin olive oil

❶Lay the bacon on the cutting board and then wrap it around the circumference of the scallop and skewer the end with one of the toothpicks. Repeat for other scallops.

❷In a smoking hot pan, place 4 scallops and sear until golden brown on both sides. The scallops should be served medium rare, but if you like scallops more well-done, place them in a pre-heated 450° oven for about 5 minutes.

❸**Cream Corn:** Place all ingredients into a pot and cook over a low heat, stirring occasionally until cream becomes thick, about 45 minutes. Season to taste.

❹Mix arugula, lemon juice and olive oil just before plating.

❺Place the cream corn in the middle of the plate and place the scallops around it. Put the arugula on top, and serve.

Photo: Tropical Dining archive

Great Chefs of **BALTIMORE**

Desserts

What could be more "Baltimore" than Lady Baltimore cake? In today's diversity of ethnic, comfort and cutting edge cuisines, you can also finish your meal with authentic Spanish flan, peanut brittle made with Baltimore's Old Bay seasoning, down home bread pudding, and creative blueberry mousse, to name a few.

Chef	Restaurant	Location
Marc Attman	Attman's Delicatessen	Corned Beef Row
Mike Broglio	Dockside	Canton
Staci Rush	Brighton's Orangerie	Inner Harbor
Michael Russell, Jr.	Vespa	Federal Hill
Emilio Sanz	Tío Pepe Restaurant	Mt. Vernon
John Shields	Gertrude's	Wyman Park
Bryan Sullivan	Formerly of Bistro 888	Fells Point
Sonny Sweetman	Abacrombie Fine Foods	Cultural District
Denise Whiting	Café Hon	Hamden

Photo: Annie Reid-Stone

Attman's Delicatessen
CHEF MARC ATTMAN

Attman's Bread Pudding

Serves 14 - 16

1 1/2 lbs	(1 1/2 loaves) egg bread, cubed
4 cups	sugar
1/2 cup	brown sugar
1 TB.	ground ginger
1 TB.	ground cinnamon
24	eggs
1 qt.	Half and Half
2 TB.	vanilla
8 TB.	butter (1 stick), melted

Topping (optional)

✓	cinnamon
✓	cooked fruit

❶ Preheat oven to 350°.

❷ Grease a 16x13-inch baking pan.

❸ Combine bread, sugars, ginger and cinnamon in large bowl.

❹ Mix eggs, Half and Half, vanilla and melted butter in separate bowl.

❺ Add dry ingredients to the wet ingredients; mix well.

❻ Bake uncovered for 20 minutes or until golden. Serve warm or cold.

❼ Can also be served with heated canned fruits sprinkled with cinnamon, as pictured.

Photo: Annie Reid-Stone

Dockside
Chef Mike Broglio

White Chocolate Bread Pudding with Dried Fruits

Serves 8

1 cup	dried fruit (cherries, cranberries, raisins)
1/2 cup	brandy
6 cups	Half & Half
4 TB.	unsalted butter
1 1/2 cups	sugar, divided
12	eggs
5 cups	dried cubed bread
1 lb.	white chocolate chips

❶ Preheat oven to 325°.

❷ Combine fruits and brandy in small sauce pan and heat slowly to simmer. When it reaches a simmer, remove from heat and set aside.

❸ In a large pot, combine Half & Half with butter and 1/2 the sugar. Heat to just boiling; then remove from heat.

❹ Combine eggs and remaining sugar in large bowl and whisk together. Slowly add cream mixture to eggs, whisking frantically. Add bread to the mixture along with the fruit and brandy.

❺ Mix thoroughly with hands, making sure the bread absorbs the egg mixture. Stir in chocolate chips.

❻ Prepare a 13"x9" baking dish (spray with Pam or similar). Pour mixture in. Bake in 325° oven for 30 minutes, or until the center is 160 degrees.

❼ Allow to cool. Loosen pudding from sides of pan and invert onto a cutting board. Cut into even pieces and serve warm with whipped cream.

❽ To re-heat, microwave individual pieces for one minute.

Photo: Annie Reid-Stone

Brighton's Orangerie
Chef Staci Rush

Blueberry Mousse

with Blueberry Stripped Genoise Cake & Blueberry Glaze

Serves 8

Cake

2½ lbs.	fine sugar
2½ lbs.	butter
1 TB.	salt
1 TB.	vanilla
2 qts.	eggs

Mousse Filling

14 oz.	sugar
1 qt.	heavy cream
9	gelatin sheets
½ cup	Chambourd liquor
8 oz.	eggs
1 lb.	blueberry puree (canned)

Blueberry Glaze

8 oz.	sugar
8 oz.	water
3 oz.	blueberry puree
✓	mint leaves for garnish

❶ Preheat oven to 300°.

❷ **Cake:** Pour sugar into the mixer to break up any lumps; add butter slowly. Add salt and vanilla, and then eggs. Sift cake flour and add in until everything is folded together. Place in buttered sheet pan and bake for 15 minutes, or until toothpick inserted into cake comes out clean.

❸ **Mousse Filling:** Cook the sugar to 248° (use a cooking thermometer). Meanwhile, whip the cream to soft peaks.

❹ Bloom gelatin in cold water to cover; drain off water; add liquor and cook on low flame until melted. Whip the eggs until frothy. When the sugar is at 248°, slowly add the eggs and continue whipping until the mixture reaches room temperature.

❺ Fold in blueberry puree and gelatin into the egg mixture by hand. Once combined, fold that mixture into the cream and place in molds.

❻ Chill in refrigerator overnight.

❼ **Blueberry Glaze:** Put all the ingredients into a pot and cook over low heat until it begins to thicken, about 30 seconds. Remove from heat and let cool.

❽ With a pastry brush, lightly brush the glaze over the chilled mousse. Then garnish the mousse with the mint leafs and serve.

Photo courtesy of Vespa

Vespa

Chef Michael Russell, Jr.

Panna Cotta

Serves 5

2 cups	heavy cream
1	vanilla bean
1	lemon, zest only
3 sheets	gelatin
1 cup	heavy cream for whipping
1 cup	powdered sugar
✓	Berries, for garnish

❶In a saucepan, combine 2 cups of heavy cream, vanilla bean and lemon zest.

❷Simmer and reduce slightly.

❸Whisk in gelatin sheets.

❹Strain and chill mixture.

❺Combine 1 cup of heavy cream and powdered sugar, whip until soft peaks form.

❻Combine cooled cream mixture with whipped cream mixture. Place into 8-ounce cups and refrigerate for about 2 hours.

❼Invert each cup on to a separate dessert plate; garnish with fresh seasonal berries.

Photo: Annie Reid-Stone

Tío Pepe Restaurant
CHEF EMILIO SANZ

Flan

Serves 4

5 1/2 oz.	sugar
4	eggs
2 1/4	cups milk
1/4	lemon, peel only
1/2 stick	cinnamon
✓	raspberries
✓	whipped cream (optional)

❶ Preheat oven to 325°.

❷ In a small saucepan on top of the stove, caramelize one third of the sugar and coat the mold with it.

❸ In a small bowl, mix together the eggs and the rest of the sugar.

❹ In a larger saucepan, heat the milk and lemon peel to just boiling. When it begins to boil, add the egg and sugar mixture. Allow the mixture to boil and then pass it through a colander into the mold.

❺ Place the mold in a water bath (bain de marie, or baño de maria). The water should come halfway up the outside wall of the mold. Place the pan into oven. Do not allow the water to boil, to avoid holes in the flan.

❻ Once the flan is set, remove from oven and allow to cool.

❼ Once cool, remove from mold. Sprinkle with cinnamon. The flan can be decorated with fresh raspberries and whipped cream.

Photo: Annie Reid-Stone

Gertrude's
CHEF JOHN SHIELDS

Lady Baltimore Cake

Serves 8 or more

Cake

1 stick	butter
2 cups	sugar
3 1/2 cups	cake flour
1 TB.	baking powder
1/4 tsp.	salt
1 tsp.	almond or vanilla extract
1 1/4	cups milk
6	egg whites

Filling and Frosting

4	egg whites
1 1/2	cup sugar
1/4	tsp. salt
1 tsp.	cream of tartar
1 tsp.	vanilla
1/2 cup	chopped raisins
3/4 cup	chopped toasted walnuts or pecans
8	dried figs, finely chopped
1 TB.	Cognac

❶Preheat oven to 350º. Grease and flour 2 9-inch round cake pans.

❷**Cake:** Beat together the butter and sugar in a mixing bowl until pale and creamy. In another bowl, sift together the flour, baking powder and salt.

❸Add the almond or vanilla extract to the milk. Add a little of the dry ingredients to the butter-sugar mixture and mix in. Then stir in a little of the milk. Alternately add the remaining dry ingredients in small amounts until both are completely incorporated. Beat until a smooth batter is formed but do not over beat.

❹Beat egg whites until stiff but not dry. Fold the egg whites into the batter, a third at a time. Pour into prepared cake pans.

❺Bake for 20 to 25 minutes or until a toothpick inserted in the middle comes out clean. Let cool in pans for 5 minutes then turn out onto a rack and cool *completely*.

❻**Filling and frosting:** Combine egg whites, sugar, salt, cream of tartar and 2/3 cup of water in top of double boiler. Beat with electric mixer over simmering water until soft peaks form, about 7 minutes. Remove from heat and beat in the vanilla. Continue beating until the frosting is stiff. Put aside half. Beat in raisins, nuts, figs and cognac into other half. Use this mixture as filling between the 2 layers of cake. Ice the entire cake with reserved frosting.

This famous Southern cake is appropriately named for our city.

Gertrude's
CHEF JOHN SHIELDS

Old Bay Peanut Brittle

Makes about 3 pounds

✓	Vegetable oil
1 TB.	Old Bay seasoning
1/2 tsp.	cayenne pepper
1 tsp.	baking soda
1 tsp.	vanilla
3 cups	sugar
1 1/4 cups	white corn syrup
1 cup	water
2 TB.	butter
4 cups	roasted peanuts, shelled and peeled

❶ Oil 3 cookie sheets well with vegetable oil.

❷ Mix the Old Bay, cayenne, baking soda and vanilla together in a small container. Set aside.

❸ Place sugar, corn syrup, water and butter in a heavy bottomed saucepan and bring to a boil. Continue cooking over high heat, brushing down any crystals that may form on the side of the pan with a pastry brush moistened with water, until the syrup reaches hard crack state (300° to 310°) on a candy thermometer.

❹ Remove from heat and add peanuts. Return saucepan to heat and bring back to a full boil.

❺ Remove from heat again and carefully (it may foam up a little) stir in the Old Bay mixture.

❻ Working quickly, pour a third of the peanut mixture onto each cookie sheet. Spread with greased spatula, distributing peanuts evenly.

❼ When the brittle is beginning to cool and congeal, but is still very hot, put on a pair of clean garden gloves. Allow to cool slightly, then grasp the sides of the brittle and gently stretch until it is very thin between the nuts.

❽ When brittle is totally cool, break into pieces. I store my brittle in small tins lined with wax paper and then covered with a tight fitting lid. It may also be stored in plastic bags. Store in a dry place.

I love my Old Bay seasoning. Of course, I (along with everyone else in the Chesapeake Bay region) was raised on it. I enjoy putting together sweet and slightly hot, spicy tastes. And that combination makes a truly enjoyable savory brittle. This is the master recipe, but feel free to play around a little. For instance, you could turn it into a pecan or hazelnut brittle and adjust the amount of the "heat" by adjusting the cayenne and Old Bay.

Take care when stirring, pouring and stretching the brittle. We are talking about a hot molten liquid. I don't normally make a lot of candy, but it really feels satisfying when you have made a batch of the brittle and are able to hand it out in small tins as a gift.

CHEF BRYAN SULLIVAN

Amaretto Cheesecake with Fresh Peach Sauce

Serves 8

1 3/4 cups	graham crackers, finely crushed
1/4 cup	chopped walnuts
1/2 tsp.	ground cinnamon
1/2 cup	margarine or butter
24 oz.	cream cheese, softened
1 cup	sugar
2	eggs
1	egg yolk
2 TB.	all purpose flour
1 tsp.	vanilla
1/4	cup milk

Fresh Peach Sauce

12 oz.	fresh peaches
✓	juice of 1/2 lemon
1/2 cup	sugar
1/2 cup	water

❶Preheat oven to 375° .

❷Combine crushed crackers, nuts and cinnamon. Stir in margarine or butter. Press mixture onto bottom of 8- or 9-inch cake pan and up sides about 2 inches.

❸In a mixing bowl, combine cream cheese, sugar, eggs, flour and vanilla. Beat with electric mixer until fluffy. Stir in milk.

❹Pour into crust-lined pan. Place pan in bain de marie (another shallow pan with water covering bottom of it). Bake at 375° for 40 or 45 minutes.

❺Remove from oven; let cool and place in refrigerator to chill overnight or at least four hours.

❻**Fresh Peach Sauce:** Puree fruit with lemon juice. Add sugar and water to desired consistency. Store in refrigerator.

❼When ready to serve, slice cheesecake into desired portions, place on your favorite dessert plate; and garnish with fresh Peach Sauce.

Photo: Annie Reid-Stone

Raspberry Ice

Serves 4

3 cups	raspberries (fresh or frozen)
1 cup	orange juice
1/2 cup	sugar
2 TB.	Chambourd liqueur (optional)
✓	additional orange juice
✓	berries, for garnish

❶In a blender, combine fruit, juice, and sugar. If desired, add liqueur.

❷Cover, and blend until smooth.

❸Press through a sieve to remove seeds.

❹Add additional orange juice to make 3 cups of the mixture.

❺Transfer to an 8x8x2-inch loaf pan, cover and freeze for 4 hours, or until firm.

❻Break frozen mixture into small chunks; transfer to a chilled bowl. Beat with an electric mixer until smooth, but not melted.

❼Return mixture to loaf pan, cover and freeze.

❽To serve, scrape across top with a spoon to make quenelles. Present in a Martini glass with a few of your favorite berries.

Photo: Annie Reid-Stone

Abacrombie Fine Foods & Accommodations

CHEF SONNY SWEETMAN

Kiln Dried Cherry Cheesecake

with Gingersnap Cookie Crust And Port Wine Sauce

Serves 4

1 cup	gingersnap cookies
2 TB.	sugar
1 tsp.	powdered ginger
3 TB.	unsalted butter, melted

Cheesecake Filling

1/2 tsp.	powdered gelatin (unflavored)
1 cup	heavy cream, divided
2 oz.	cream cheese, softened
1/4 cup	sour cream
2 TB.	sugar
1/4 tsp.	vanilla extract
1/4	vanilla bean, split/scraped

Kiln Dried Cherry Topping

2 cups	Port wine
1 cup	sugar
1	star anise
1/4	vanilla bean, split/scraped
1	cinnamon stick
1/4 tsp.	ground allspice
1 cup	dried cherries
1 tsp.	orange zest

❶Preheat oven to 350°. In food processor, combine gingersnaps, sugar and ginger on "pulse." Slowly add melted butter, until crust comes together. Press mixture in bottoms/sides of 4 individual tartlet molds.

❷Bake for 10 minutes, then cool on a wire rack.

❸**Filling:** In medium bowl, sprinkle the gelatin over 1/4 cup of heavy cream. Allow the gelatin to soften for 5 minutes. Meanwhile, in small saucepan over medium heat, bring 1/2 cup cream and cream cheese to simmer. Whisk until mixture is smooth and fully melted.

❹Add mixture to the bowl with softened gelatin and whisk until the gelatin dissolves. Strain through a fine sieve into a clean bowl; let cool to room temperature.

❺With electric mixer, whip the remaining heavy 1/4 cup cream, sour cream, sugar, vanilla extract and vanilla pulp in new bowl until mixture holds medium peaks. Fold a third of it into the cream cheese mixture, then fold in the remaining whipped cream mixture in two additions. Pour the filling into the cooled tart shells and refrigerate until set, about 4 hours.

❻**Topping:** In a small saucepan, bring the port wine, sugar, star anise, vanilla pulp, and the spices to a simmer. Reduce the heat to very low and simmer. Add the dried cherries and allow to plump and thicken the liquid until it coats the back of a spoon.

❼Remove from heat and remove whole spices. Refrigerate. When cool, fold in orange zest.

❽Top the cheese cakes with the cherry mixture and serve.

Photo: Annie Reid-Stone

Bread Pudding with Caramel Sauce

Serves 10-12

1 loaf	white bread (24 ozs), cubed (cheap brand is fine)
1 cup	light brown sugar
1 cup	white sugar
10	large eggs
3 TB.	pure vanilla extract (not imitation)
2 TB.	cinnamon
$5\frac{1}{2}$ cups	whole milk
1 stick	butter, melted

Caramel Sauce:

$1\frac{1}{4}$ cups	light brown sugar
1 stick	butter
2 cups	heavy cream

❶ Preheat oven to 400°.

❷ In a greased $11\frac{3}{4}$ x $9\frac{1}{4}$ x $2\frac{1}{2}$ inch aluminum roasting pan, add the cubed bread.

❸ In a bowl, whisk together brown and white sugars, eggs, vanilla and cinnamon. Add milk and melted butter.

❹ Gently pour the mixture over bread cubes, covering all the bread (do not stir the bread with the mixture as this will create a denser product).

❺ Bake at 400° for 45 minutes, then lower the heat to 350° and bake another 15 minutes.

❻ Allow to cool so bread pudding can set.

❼ **Caramel Sauce:** Mix all ingredients in a small saucepan and cook until mixture boils and sugar is melted. Serve with fresh whipped cream.

❽ To serve, place slice of pudding on serving plate; pour sauce over it.

Notes

Index of Chefs

Index of Chefs

Index of Chefs

Notes

Recipe Index

Recipe Index

Recipe Index

Recipe Index

Notes

Notes

Notes

Featured Restaurants

The Great Chefs of Baltimore cook in these restaurants. You'll want to try more of their delicious dishes.

Abacrombie Fine Food
58 West Biddle Street
Baltimore, MD 21201
410-244-7227

Attman's Delicatessen
1019 E. Lombard Street
Baltimore, MD 21202
410-563-2666

Restaurant "b"
1501 Bolton Street
Baltimore, MD 21207
410-383-8600

Babalu Grill
Restaurant Row @ Market Place
32 Market Place
Baltimore, MD 21202
410-234-9898

Baldwin's Station
7618 Main Street
Sykesville, MD. 21274
410-795-1041

The Bicycle
1444 Light Street
Baltimore, MD 21230
410-234-1900

Blue Sea Grill
Restaurant Row @ Market Place
614 Water Street
Baltimore, MD 21202
410-837-7300

The Brass Elephant
924 N. Charles Street
Baltimore, MD 21201
410-547-8480

The Brewer's Art
1106 N. Charles Street
Baltimore, MD 21201
410-547-6925

Brighton's Orangerie
InterContinental Harbor Court
550 Light Street
Baltimore, MD 21202
410-234-0550

Charleston
1000 Lancaster Street
Baltimore, MD 21202
410-332-7373

The Chameleon Café
4341 Harford Road
Baltimore, MD 21214
410-254-2376

Chiapparelli's Restaurant
237 S. High Street
Baltimore, MD 21202
410-837-0309

Corks
1026 S. Charles Street
Baltimore, MD. 21230
410-752-3810

Crossroads Restaurant
Radisson Cross Keys Inn
5100 Falls Road
Baltimore, MD 21210
410-532-6900

Dalesio's of Little Italy
829 Eastern Avenue
Baltimore, MD 21202
410-539-1965

Da Mimmo's Restaurant
217 S. High Street
Baltimore, MD. 21202
410-727-6876

Dionysus Restaurant & Lounge
8 East Preston Street
Baltimore, MD 21201
410-244-1020

Dockside
3301 Boston Street
Baltimore, MD 21224
410-276-8900

Donna's Café
2 West Madison Street
Baltimore, MD 21201
410-385-0180
and others

George's
Peabody Court Hotel
612 Cathedral Street
Baltimore, MD 21201
410-727-1314

Gertrude's at Museum of Art
10 Art Museum Drive
Baltimore, MD 21218
410-889-3399

Gibby's
22 West Padonia Road
Baltimore, MD
410-560-0703

Grill 700 at Marriott Hotel
700 Aliceanna Street
Baltimore, MD 21202
410-385-3000

Featured Restaurants

Hampton's at Intercontinental
Harbor Court Hotel
550 Light Street
Baltimore, MD 21202
410-234-0550

The Helmand Restaurant
806 N. Charles Street
Baltimore, MD21201
410-752-0311

IXIA
518 N. Charles Street
Baltimore, MD 31201
410-727-1800

Kali's Court
1606 Thames Street
Baltimore MD 21231
410-276-4700

La Scala Ristorante
1012 Eastern Avenue
Baltimore, MD 21202
410-783-9209

Mezze
1606 Thames Street
Baltimore, MD 21231
410-563-7600

Obrycki's
1727 East Pratt Street
Baltimore, MD 21231
410-732-6399

Phillips Harborplace Restaurant
301 Light Street
Baltimore, MD 21224
410-685-6600

Red Fish
845 S. Montford Avenue
Baltimore, MD 21224
410-524-1454

Ruth's Chris Steakhouse-Pier 5
711 Eastern Avenue, Pier 5
Baltimore, MD 21202
410-230-0033

Ryan's Daughter
600 Belvedere Square
Baltimore, MD 21212
410-464-1000

Sabatino's
901 Fawn Street
Little Italy
Baltimore, MD 21202
410-727-9414

Shula's Steak House
Wyndham Baltimore Hotel
101 W. Fayette Street
Baltimore, MD 21202
410-385-6601

Tapas Teatro
1711 N. Charles Street
Baltimore, MD 21201
410-332-0110

Tío Pepe Restaurant
10 East Franklin Street
Baltimore, MD 21201
410-539-4675

Vespa
1117 S. Charles Street
Baltimore, MD 21230
410-385-0355

Vin Restaurant
1 East Joppa Road
Towson, MD
410-637-0797

Window's Restaurant
Renaissance Harborplace Hotel
202 E. Pratt Street
Baltimore MD 21201
410-685-8439

Zodiac
1726 N. Charles Street
Baltimore, MD 21201
410-727-8815

Café Hon
1002 West 36th Street
Baltimore, MD 21211
410-243-1230

Roy's Restaurant
720 Aliceanna Street
Baltimore, MD 21202
410-659-0099